THE INTERPRETATION OF THE BIBLE IN THE MISHNAH

THE INTERPRETATION OF THE BIBLE IN THE MISHNAH

by

SAMUEL ROSENBLATT, Ph.D.

Lecturer on Jewish Literature
The Johns Hopkins University

WIPF & STOCK · Eugene, Oregon

Wipf and Stock Publishers
199 W 8th Ave, Suite 3
Eugene, OR 97401

The Interpretation of the Bible in the Mishnah
By Rosenblatt, Samuel
ISBN 13: 978-1-60608-030-6
Publication date 7/10/2008
Previously published by Johns Hopkins Press, 1935

To Claire

in love and affection

FOREWORD

On issuing this little volume, the first of a series of monographs which, it is hoped, will embrace the entire field of Tannaitic literature, I must unburden myself of my indebtedness to all those persons who have, in one way or another, been of assistance to me. I wish to render thanks to my teacher Professor Louis Ginzberg of the Jewish Theological Seminary of America for his valued advice and guidance in the conception as well as the execution of this work, to my friend and superior Professor W. F. Albright, head of the Oriental Seminary of The Johns Hopkins University, for his kind stimulation and encouragement, and finally to the subscribers to the Lectureship in Jewish Literature at the The Johns Hopkins University and others whose financial support has made it possible for this essay to see the light of day.

August 1, 1935

Samuel Rosenblatt

TABLE OF CONTENTS

KEY TO THE ABBREVIATIONS AND OTHER SIGNS.

Tannaitic Sources:

M	Mekhilta of Rabbi Ishmael
MS	Mekhilta of Rabbi Simon ben Jochai, edition Hoffmann
Sa	Sifra
Se	Sifre on Numbers and Deuteronomy
SZ	Sifre Zutta, edition Horovitz
MT	Midrash Tannaim, edition Hoffmann

(Note: the quotations from all these sources are always ad locum unless otherwise indicated)

Tos	Tosefta, edition Zuckermandel
Br	Boraitha
Brs	Boraithas

(Note: quotations from the Mishnah or Tosefta are always given by the chapter, which is indicated by a Roman numeral, and paragraph, which is indicated by an Arabic numeral. The Boraithas are quoted according to their place in the Talmudim q. v.)

Amoraic Sources:

b	Babylonian Talmud quoted according to the pagination of the standard printed editions
j	Jerusalem Talmud, ad locum, unless otherwise indicated, when the chapter and halakha is quoted according to the Krotoschin edition

Translations:

O	Targum Onkelos, edition Berliner
PJ	Targum Pseudo-Jonathan, edition Ginsburger
S	Septuagint, edition Swete
V (when used alone)	Vulgate, edition Bredt, Leipzig, 1838
Pš	Pshitto, London edition
J	Targum Jonathan on the Prophets, מקראות גדולות
T	Targum on the Hagiographa, מקראות גדולות
anon.	anonymous author
R	Rabbi
b	ben (when occurring in connection with a proper name)
||	parallel to
=	"is" or "equals"
≍	is equivalent to

Quotations from the commentaries of Rashi (on the Mishnah) or of Malbim (on the Bible) are ad locum unless otherwise indicated.

m.	masculine
f.	feminine

Books of the Bible:

Gen	Genesis
Ex	Exodus
Lev	Leviticus
Num	Numbers
Dt	Deuteronomy
Jos	Joshua
Jud	Judges
I and II Sam	First and Second Samuel
I and II Kings	First and Second Kings
Is	Isaiah
Jer	Jeremiah
Ez	Ezekiel
Hosea	
Joel	
Amos	
Micah	
Zech	Zechariah
Mal	Malachi
Ps	Psalms
Pr	Proverbs
Job	
Cant	Canticles
Ruth	
Lam	Lamentations
Eccl	Ecclesiastes
Ezra	
I and II Chr	First and Second Chronicles

(Note: the chapters are always indicated by a Roman, the verses by an Arabic numeral.)

Treatises of the Mishnah, Toseftah and Talmudim

Ber	Berakhoth
Peah	
Kil	Kil'ayim
Shebi	Shebi'ith
Ter	Terumoth
Maas Sh	Ma'asser Sheni
Ḥallah	
Bik	Bikkurim
Sabb	Sabbath
Pes	Pesachim
Sheḳ	Sheḳalim
Yoma	
Sukk	Sukkah
R Hash	Rosh Hashanah

Taan	Ta'anith
Meg	Megillah
M Ḳaṭ	Mo'ed Katan
Ḥag	Ḥagigah
Yab	Yabmuth
Ket	Kethuboth
Ned	Nedarim
Naz	Nazir
Soṭ	Soṭah
Giṭṭ	Giṭṭin
Ḳidd	Ḳiddushin
B Ḳam	Baba Ḳamma
B Meṣ	Baba Meṣi'a
Snh	Sanhedrin
Makk	Makkoth
Shebu	Shebu'oth
Ed	'Eduyoth
Ab Zar	'Abodah Zarah
Ab	Aboth
Hor	Horayoth
Zeb	Zebachim
Men	Menachoth
Ḥull	Ḥullin
Bekh	Bekhoroth
Arakh	'Arakhin
Tem	Temurah
Ker	Kerithoth
Tam	Tamid
Midd	Middoth
Neg	Nega'im
Parah	
Miḳw	Miḳwa'oth
Makhsh	Makhshirin
Zab	Zabim
Yad	Yadayim
Uḳṣ	'Uḳṣin

I

Literal Meaning in the Bible Exegesis of the Mishnah

In an essay that appeared in 1879 and was entitled "Beiträge zur hebräischen Grammatik im Talmud und Midrasch" the celebrated Jewish scholar Abraham Berliner set out to prove the thesis that the rabbinic expositors of the Bible were by no means, as was commonly believed, "lacking in a sense for grammar", and that, even if they were not strictly scientific in their approach of the subject, valuable contributions to the history of Hebrew lexicography and grammar and even of grammatical terminology are to be found in their comments.[1] Fourteen years after Berliner's disclosures had come to light, L. Dobschütz[2] showed that this statement, that had been made chiefly with reference to the Amoraim, applied particularly to their predecessors the Tannaim. The testimony of these and other authorities[3] regarding the philological endowments of the rabbinic expositors makes desirable a thorough and systematic investigation of the rabbinic exegesis of the Bible, with a view especially of ascertaining how the rabbis conceived the פשט or literal meaning of the scriptural text, what methods they used in establishing it and what terms they employed in their philological remarks.

Such a task has not yet been undertaken. The work of Georg Aicher on the Old Testament in the Mishna,[4] which made its appearance in 1906, fails to note the deeper philological implications of the Mishnaic interpretations of the Bible. Malbim's monumental commentary on the Mekhilta, Sifra and Sifre,[5] again, while it is extremely useful, because of its critical insight into the nature of rabbinic exegesis, for a synthesis of rabbinic Bible interpretation, suffers, on account of its character as a running commentary, from the want of a convenient arrangement requisite for the mastery of so complicated a subject. Besides that it goes to the extreme of attempting to reduce every

Tannaitic exposition of the biblical text, however forced or far-fetched, to פשט.

An objective and critical examination of rabbinic exegesis of the Bible is, therefore, still a desideratum. Hence the present effort which was suggested and sponsored by my teacher Prof. Louis Ginzberg of the Jewish Theological Seminary of America. It is intended to be the first of a series of monographs each dealing with one of the major compilations of Tannaitic, to be followed by those of Amoraic, literature. Our reasons for commencing with the Mishnah rather than with the more specifically exegetical works of the Tannaim are, besides the more manageable size of the material, the facts that as the authoritative text-book of the Talmudical academies it is in a better state of preservation than other collections, and that, having been widely commented on in both Talmudim, we possess, in the absence of authentic originals, more checks for it than for the less frequently discussed midrashim.[6]

Before attempting to discover how the Mishnaic expositors conceived the literal meaning or פשט of the Bible it is necessary to note what they understood by the term פשט or literal meaning. That that term could not have been used by them in exactly the same sense in which it is employed today is beyond dispute, for the construction which is put upon an ancient text such as the Scriptures already were in the days of the Tannaim is conditioned by the standards of criticism and the general view of history that is held by the student, and those that prevailed at the time of the Mishnaic exegetes were not the same as those that are current among modern Bible scholars. The Mishnaic interpreters of Scripture did not, for example, entertain the possibility of a composite authorship of the Pentateuch, a theory upheld by most Bible critics of our own age. All the five books of Moses were assumed by them to hail from one source. This assumption compelled them, on the one hand, to endeavor to reconcile all contradictions,[7] while on the other it left them free to utilize the expressions of one book or context in order to illuminate those of another.[8] How that must have affected their literal exegesis can readily be seen.

The Tannaitic exegetes differed, furthermore, from modern

Bible interpreters in that they recognized no development in either language, or religious conceptions. No distinction existed for them between the dialect of the Prophets and the Hagiographa and that employed by the Pentateuch. Hence the connotation expressions had in the former would be their significance in the latter.[9] The religion of the heroes of the Bible was the Law of Moses with which their conduct always had to be in harmony. Its philosophy, i. e. the philosophy of the Bible, was according to them identical with that of rabbinic Judaism which regarded as the ideal occupation of man the study of Torah and the fulfillment of its precepts.[10] When the Bible speaks of "the congregation of God"[11] or "His band that He has established on earth"[12] or "the God-fearing"[13] "that think of His name"[14] it refers to students of Torah.[15] "Silent meditation"[16] that deserves reward is meditation over the Law.[17] The "righteous"[18] "whose hope is in God"[19] are those who live according to the precepts of the Torah.[20] It is in keeping with this practice of imputing to the Bible and biblical characters rabbinic conceptions that the patriarch Abraham could be thought to have observed the entire Torah before it was given at Sinai,[21] that Boaz was pictured as a legislator,[22] and the highpriest Joyada as a darshan who interpreted the Pentateuch in the typical rabbinic manner,[23] and the conduct of saints and heroes regarded as the norm to follow.[24]

Another point that must be borne in mind if we wish to obtain a correct idea of what the Bible exegetes of the Mishnah understood by פשט is that to them the Pentateuch was, outside of its narrative portions, a code of laws and that if they applied, especially to the legal sections, a strict and literalistic construction, they pursued a policy followed by most jurists in reading legal documents.

One of the principles observed in the interpretation of legal instruments is that their stipulations cannot be made to exceed the narrowest meaning of the phraseology. In rabbinic literature this principle is expressed in the sentence of תפשת מרובה לא תפשת תפשת מועט תפשת.[25] Applied to the text of Scripture that meant that unqualified plurals never equalled more than "two",[26] that injunctions with reference to certain enumerated objects or persons were not to be extended to others,[27] that precepts were to be fulfilled exactly in the form stated[28] to the exclusion of any other,[29] that the order of statement possessed significance the item coming first being preferred,[30] except if it was proven that the order was immaterial.[31] The construction of generic singulars[32] and plurals[33] as numerical was merely an extension of this principle.

The assumption underlying the narrow construction of the text of legal documents is that the wording is precise and definite. Broader meanings must be specifically indicated either by repetition or the use of pleonastic expressions, or otherwise. Following this line of reasoning the exegetes of the Mishnah attached special significance to redundancies[34] and pleonasms.[35] The recurrence of an expression[36] denoted, in their opinion, emphasis either restricting or extending its application. A superfluous synonym,[37] a duplication of the same thought[38] in different words pointed to a broader meaning. Not all the Tannaim, however, concurred in such interpretations.[39] Some preferred to regard such latitudes of expression as instances in which, to use a maxim of Rabbi Ishmael's, the Torah employed the inexact language of men דברה תורה כלשון בני אדם.[40]

To the principles of interpretation used in the reading of legal instruments that were applied by the Tannaim in the exposition of the Pentateuchal text must be added the rule of סמוכין, i. e. the theory that the characteristics appertaining to one member of a series or of items mentioned side by side and having a certain affinity belong also to the others.[41]

A final distinguishing feature of the exegesis of the Tannaim which differentiates it from that of modern Bible scholars is the fact that the former did not practice emendation. Not that they always followed the massoretic accentuation, or sentence division, or that metathesis of consonants or the mental rearrangement of verses was shunned by them. This was not the case.[42] Yet was it imperturbable law with them that the letter of the scriptural word must not be touched. No violence was to be done to the text. Difficulties were to be explained.[43] They were not to be resolved by cutting the Gordian knot.

With these reservations the exegetes of the Mishnah may be

said to have engaged in what would today be called literal exegesis. That they were interested in discovering the פשט or simple meaning of the text is evident not only from certain verbal remarks[44] but also from their practice in the Mishnah. It is possible to distinguish several types of comments that fit very well into the category of פשט or literal interpretation. First of all there are to be included in this class the definitions (of biblical terms) that are labelled by the formulae איזהו,[45] זה,[46] האמור בתורה,[47] כמשמעו,[48] כלומר,[49] אינו אומר,[50] אין . . . אלא.[51] A second group falling within this division is comprised by nearly all those cases in which a biblical passage cited in the Mishnah has been variously interpreted by the Tannaim.[52] The fact that two or more different constructions are put on the same expression is, as I. H. Weiss observes in his History of Jewish Tradition,[53] a sure indication that the halakha or the agada was the result of the exegesis or midrash, not its cause, and that we deal here, so far as the rabbinic expositors were concerned, with literal exegesis or פשט, however forced and far-fetched the interpretation may seem to modern exegetes. Were the biblical text quoted merely as an אסמכתא, i. e. as the support of a preconceived opinion, how does it happen that two divergent views derive their authority from the same source?[54] Furthermore, the controversy clarifies the issues, for wherever there is a conflict of opinions, there must be a common denominator around which the disagreement centers.

If we deduct the exegetical material constituted by these two classes as well as those cases in which the Bible is quoted only for the sake of application[55] or in order to bring out the general implications[56] of the text, not for the sake of textual exegesis, whether explicit or implicit, i. e. those instances which belong to what Aicher calls the field of "Schriftanwendung" rather than that of "Schriftauslegung", we obtain a third category of examples of literal exegesis or פשט in the Mishnah.[57]

We are prepared, now that we have defined the limits of our investigation, to examine more closely the exegesis of the Bible in the Mishnah. To facilitate the examination we shall divide the material into lexicographical, grammatical and historical-critical. This is to be followed by a summary of the methodology of Mishnaic Bible exegesis. The concluding chapter will attempt an evaluation of the Bible interpretation of the Mishnah. In the appendix, finally, will be given a translation into English, on the basis of the Mishnaic expositions, of all the passages commented on textually.

II

Materials for Biblical Lexicography in the Bible Exegesis of the Mishnah.

Despite the failure of any mention of vowel signs in the Mishnah or other Tannaitic sources it seems quite certain that the reading of the Old Testament current today was already firmly established and, so far as the Mishnah at least was concerned, no attempts were made to change the vocalization. Of the four instances reported in the Mishnah in which emendations in pronunciation were believed to have been made, two[1] have been proven conclusively by Malbim to have been cases of interpretation, the third[2] appears to be merely a mnemonic device, while the fourth[3] was, as Geiger has pointed out in his Urschrift, a return to the original version which had been altered for reasons of decency. In our investigation of the lexicographical material contained in the Mishnah we are dealing, then, with a lexicography that presupposes a text resembling in every essential the one that lies before us and it is unnecessary to assume any variations that might have prompted the peculiar exegesis of its exponents.

Before we list the actual definitions of the vocabulary of the Bible expressed or implied in the exegesis of the Mishnah, it is well to be oriented in the philological principles underlying them. It is evident from such etymologies as שעטנז[4] = שוע וטווי ונוז i. e. שע+ט+נז[5] that the exegetes of the Mishnah subscribed to the theory, that was maintained until the 11th century, of biliteral and even uniliteral roots.[6] This applied of course to all roots now construed as having one or two of the weak letters י, ו, ה, א, as geminates or as primae or tertiae נ. In other words these weak or duplicate letters were not considered as part of the root. Orthographically some of them were interchangeable. Thus א

might be replaced by ה[7] or ו by א[8] at the end of a word. An affinity was certainly believed to have existed between them, for roots, however they might be differentiated in their weak letters, having the same strong radicals were regarded as equivalent[9] or at least synonymous. There is also evidence in the Mishnah of the assumption of such a kinship between the gutturals א and ע,[10] and the linguals ל and נ,[11] and of the recognition that prosthetic מ is not always part of the root.[12]

In line with this general tendency towards the reduction of the number of radicals is the breaking up of complex into simpler forms. Five-letter words were believed to be of a composite nature and were defined as such.[13] This principle was applied by the Tannaim even to four- and three-letter roots[14] but of this we have no definite example in the Mishnah.

If the case of שעטנז, which was construed as a composite of three Hebrew roots, can be regarded as typical, then the Mishnaic exegetes of the Bible did not assume any of the foreign-looking terms of the Old Testament to be of non-Hebrew or at least non-Semitic origin.[15] Likewise there is apparent in the Bible exegesis of the Mishnah a disinclination for hapaxlegomena. Rare expressions are shown rather to be related to familiar roots.[16] Instead of suspecting another root metathesis is at times assumed not only within the same[17] word but between the letters of two adjacent words.[18] Homonymous roots were, it seems, conceived as identical.[19]

Having obtained an insight into the theories regarding the structure of roots entertained by the Bible exegetes of the Mishnah the next question we must ask ourselves is how they were equipped for the definition of biblical terms. A study of the Mishnah itself reveals that they were well acquainted with ground meanings of roots, that they recognized ambiguities, that they had at their disposal traditions concerning the significance of unusual expressions, that they were assisted by popular usage of the Hebrew language which in the schoolroom, at least, was still a living tongue, and that they were able to make use, for comparison, among other Semitic dialects of at least the Aramaic vernacular which was current in Palestine at the time. They knew for example that the primary significance of אחר is "to be behind another",[20] of דבר "word",[21] that the ground meaning of כון is "to be straight",[22] of הניף "to swing back and forth", of הרים "to lift up",[23] that the phrase על פי is made up of the preposition על and the noun פה "mouth",[24] that ענה denoted at bottom "repeat"[25] and עשה "to act",[26] that רגלים "times" is derived from רגל "foot"[27] and קללה from קל "to be light",[28] and עולה from עלה "go up".[29] It is expressly noted by one and the same authority that אשם might stand for "guilt offering" or "debt" owed to the sanctuary for misappropriation of its property,[30] that אפרוחים may denote full-fledged chicks as well as chicks not fully fledged, and ביצים hatchable as well as non-hatchable eggs,[31] that גדי may be applied to the young of wild as well as domesticated animals,[32] that דבר in the sense of "thing" connotated at times a "substantiated matter"[33] and at other times "something",[34] that הונה may refer to mental as well as material oppression,[35] that הלך עם is used in a figurative as well as literal sense,[36] that the particle זה[37] may be construed either a demonstrative or an enclitic of place, that יום may stand either for day as contrasted with night or the complete diurnal cycle,[38] that what is meant by יום אחד "one and the same day" depends upon how the day is reckoned and there is a difference,[39] that מבן . . . ועד can be interpreted either as "above . . . . . years" or "from. . . . . . years and above",[40] that נפש בנפש may mean life for "life taken" or life for "life condemned",[41] that צאן is the designation for the sheep species as well as for Kleinvieh in general,[42] that על in some places means "on" and in others "near",[43] that שבת is both "Sabbath" and "week"[44] and that תמיד is applied not only to what continues without interruption but also to what is constant.[45] Of unusual terms the meaning of which they were able to define only because they were at the source we can point with certainty to מאד "wealth"[46] קטורות[47] "unroofed" and עוללות[48] "gleanings". Of words expressly illuminated by popular usage may be mentioned קללת אלהים[49] and דק[50] and there is at least the hapaxlegomenon דמע[51] which is interpreted in the light of the Aramaic root "to mix" rather than in that of the Hebrew "to weep".

Such was the linguistic equipment with which the Bible exegetes of the Mishnah approached their task. What critical acumen they exercised in their lexicography will be discussed later. Here let it suffice to say that, being primarily expounders of the law for the practical purposes of life, or moralists who looked to the Sacred Scriptures for guidance, they were not always content with the simple sense of the text. They sought deeper intimations in the Bible and they found them either in the ground meanings of derived forms, the secondary uses of expressions employed in the text in their primary sense, or in the ambiguities of words of equivocal meaning. Thus the use of the expression דבר in connection with the laws of the year release and that of the murderer, instead of some unequivocal term, indicated to them that these laws are not complied with unless the words "I release" and "I am a murderer" are spoken,[52] and the origin of the word עולה that once the holocaust is on the altar it is not to go down.[53] From על פי שנים עדים they inferred that the witnesses must warn the would-be-culprit and also that the testimony must be personal, not mediate,[54] from כליל, which in its secondary meaning denotes holocaust, used in connection with the banished city,[55] that he who destroys the latter brings a holocaust to God,[56] from עמו in the injunction[57] עזב תעזב עמו that the passerby is to assist the owner of the beast borne down by its burden but not do all the work himself,[58] from רגלים that the trip up to the temple must be made on foot.[59]

Then again there were given to the vocabulary of the Bible neo-Hebrew connotations prevalent at the time of the Tannaim. Thus by בריתי[60] they understood the covenant of circumcision,[61] גר[62] was always "proselyte",[63] ערל[64] "gentile",[65] רבים[66] "a majority",[67] תורתי[68] the Torah,[69] משפט[70] is once interpreted as "court procedure"[71] and מקום[72] is used as in rabbinic Hebrew as a synonym for God.[73]

On the whole, however, the Mishnaic exegetes remained within the bounds of biblical Hebrew in their definitions. Thus for example אלהים "judges"[74] has its counterpart in Ex XXII 7 ff.; אסף "to bury"[75] in Gen XXV 8 and 17, XXXV 29, XLIX 33; הגדיל[76] "to make great" in the quantitative sense in I Sam XX 41; דוה "menstruant" in Lev XII 2; התעמר[78] "to use as a slave" in Dt XXI 14; מקדש[79] "holy city" in Amos VII 13; שקץ regard unclean like a creeping thing in Lev XI 43 אל תשקצו

ולא תטמאו את נפשותיכם בכל השרץ 44 || את נפשתיכם בכל השרץ;[80] רצון "will"[81] in II Chr XV 15; רעה "misfortune"[82] in Ex X 10; בראשון "on Nisan"[83] in Gen VIII 13.

These interpretations did not always fit the context, but over against those that did not there are, as a consultation of the list compiled in our appendix indicates, many that did; and again, as will readily be seen there, passages that were expounded by some authorities unnaturally were explained by others according to their simple literal meaning.

III

Materials towards a Biblical Grammar in the Bible Exegesis of the Mishnah

From the biblical lexicography of the Mishnah let us now turn to grammar. As has been remarked at the beginning of this investigation the scientific idiom employed by modern philologians was, so far as can be ascertained from the sources, unknown to the Bible exegetes of the Mishnah. This does not mean, however, that they were unfamiliar with the phenomena of language generally included under grammar and syntax, or that they were unable to express themselves clearly in this regard. On the contrary there are many indications in the Mishnah itself pointing to a fine understanding of the niceties of speech coming under this heading, as well as rudiments of a technical terminology. Following are the data on which this assertion is based:

As to the verb,

of the various forms the קַל denotes simple, spontaneous, not causative, action. This is expressed by contrasting it with the הִפְעִיל as "כי ינח" ולא שיניחוהו;[1]

the פִּעֵל may have a denominative and causative force as in שקץ תשקצנו[2] which is obviously translated "thou shalt regard it (unclean) like a שקץ";[3]

the פִּעֵל expresses transitive, not stative, action as appears from אין קורין מעוות אלא למי שהיה מתוקן בתחלה ונתעוות;[4]

the הִפְעִיל is definitely causative: e. g. אשר יעשה[5] is construed as שיורה[6] לעשות;
the הָפְעַל, again, is considered transitive according to the remark[7]: אם יש משקה טמא בתורה עד שיתכון ויתן שנאמר „וכי יֻתַּן מים על זרע"[8]

Of the tenses,
the perfect may express future action, i. e. the prophetic future, as in בלע המות לנצח[9] concerning which is made the remark אבל לעתיד לבא הוא אומר;[10]
the imperfect of even the qal of stative verbs is regarded as active, in comparison with the participle which is stative only, at least by R Aḳiba who says of כל אשר בתוכו יטמא[11]: "אינו אומר טמא, אלא יטמא, לטמא אחרים";[12]
its employment to express future action is clear in כל ישראל יש להם חלק לעולם הבא שנאמר . . . לעולם יירשו . . .[13]

As to persons:
the third person singular (especially of passive verbs) may be used impersonally to refer to the thought contained in a whole clause rather than a personal subject as, for example ונעלם ממנו in או בנבלת שרץ טמא ונעלם ממנו והוא טמא[14] which is made to refer either to או (אשר תגע) בנבלת שרץ טמא[15] or to והוא טמא.[16]

The *infinitive* absolute used alone before the finite verb intensifies the action: e. g. השב תשיבם,[17] עזב תעזב,[18] שלח תשלח,[19] which are interpreted as אפילו ארבעה וחמשה פעמים[20] and פדה תפדה[21] which which is taken to indicate that המפריש פדיון בנו ואבד חייב באחריותו.[22] If a negative intervenes, as e. g. in והפדה לא נפדתה,[23] it denotes, according to R Aḳiba,[24] action begun but not completed.

The infinitive construct with the preposition ב prefixed and the pronominal suffixes affixed may express either manner or time. Thus בשכבך ובקומך[25] is interpreted by the Shammaiites: בערב כל אדם יטו ויקראו ובבקר יעמדו and by the Hillelites: בשעה שבני אדם שוכבים ובשעה שבני אדם עומדים.[26]

The infinitive construct with the preposition ל prefixed is used independently sometimes to denote compulsion as in אחרי רבים להטת.[27] Used dependently it may express purpose—therefore future action—, as להרע או להיטיב in או נפש כי תשבע . . . להרע או להיטיב[28] from which is derived the thought that אינו חייב אלא על העתיד לבא.[29] In the phrase לאמר[30] it expresses manner.[31] It is, however, also construed by one expositor[32] as an ordinary (verbal) noun in the dative.

The *participle* passive used as the predicate in a nominal sentence without a finite verb could denote future action. E. g. ברוך in 'ברוך הגבר אשר יבטח בה[33] is interpreted as כל מי שצריך ליטול ואינו נוטל אינו מת מן הזקנה עד שיפרנס אחרים משלו.[34]

The active participle may be used with the preposition ב in place of an abstract noun to denote attendant circumstances as e. g. בטמא in לא בערתי ממנו בטמא[35] which is interpreted בטומאה.[36]

Pertaining to the *government of the verb* it is implied that the subject of the infinitive construct might also be construed as its object, like e. g. אחיך with דרש in עד דרש אחיך אותו.[37]
The object of a participle used as subject in a sentence may be construed also as the object of the verb as e. g. הבערה in שלם ישלם המבעיר את הבערה[38] which one authority interprets "that the amount of compensation depends on the extent of the brand",[39] i. e. שלם ישלם את הבערה.

The agent of a passive verb may sometimes be a noun introduced by the preposition ב as e. g. בישראל in ונקרא שמו בישראל בית חלוץ הנעל,[40] according to R Judah, who remarks thereon: מצוה על כל העומדים שם לאמר חלוץ הנעל.[41]

In regard to *the noun* it has already been observed previously that there was a tendency to construe generic singulars and plurals as numerical.[42] This rendering was, however, by no means universal. There were *singulars* that were recognized as *generic*, e. g. זכר ונקבה in זכר ונקבה בראם[43] according to the Shammaiites, who interpret this verse "male or female he created them"[44] and therefore deduce that the minimum for procreation is two males;[45]
or as *collectives*, e. g. תמורתו in והיה הוא ותמורתו,[46] according to one authority, who states it may stand for even a hundred.[47]

There were *plurals* that were conceived as *generic*, e. g. ביצים . . . אפרוחים in כי יקרא קן צפור . . . אפרוחים או ביצים[48] which were regarded merely as descriptive of the nature of the קן צפור, for even if אין שם אלא אפרוח או ביצה אחת חייב לשלח,[49]
פרו ורבו[50] which are taken to apply only to the male,[50a],
ימים in והימים הראשונים יפלו,[51] which to one authority does not imply the existence of "first" days.[52]

The uses of the plural form for units spread over an area, i. e. plural of *extension*, was also noted:
e. g. ימים in ולמקוה המים קרא ימים,[53] according to R Judah, who remarks that this refers to the Great Sea which has been so called because יש בו מיני ימים הרבה,[54]
דמי in קול דמי אחיך צועקים מן האדמה[55], which indicated according to one interpretation that his blood was cast over the trees and the stones.[56]

Repetition was recognized as another way of expressing the plural idea, e. g. אמן, אמן in ואמרה האשה אמן אמן[57] is understood by one expositor not in a strict[58] but rather in a distributive sense.[59]

The technical names used for singular and plural in the Mishnah are מיוחד[60] *and* הרבה.[61]

The *determination* of the noun *by the article* was known to the Bible exegetes of the Mishnah. The article had either a *distinctive* function, e. g. הכהן in ונגש הכהן ודבר אל העם,[62] which was interpreted as "The Priest",[63] or המשפט in אל כן לא יקומו רשעים במשפט,[64] which R Nehemiah interprets as "The Judgment",
or a *generic* force, as e. g. הקדש in ונתן לכהן את הקדש[66] which R Akiba interprets: כל הראוי להיות קדש,[67]
or it has a *demonstrative* value, referring to something mentioned before, e. g. R Eliezer's rendering of הקדש as קדש שאכל,[68]
or to something to be mentioned, e. g. the construction of המשפט according to the colleagues of R. Nehemiah[69] who consider this as parallel to the following עדת צדיקים.

The *genitive* relationship is another mode of the determination of the noun that figures prominently in the Bible exegesis of the Mishnah. A genitive with a verbal noun was construed as subjective, objective or explicative, with ordinary nouns as possessive or descriptive.
Illustrations of the first class are:
לרצונו[70] whence אין מתכפר לו עד שיתרצה,[71] i. e. "his will",
דבר הרוצח[72] whence אף הוא היה מדבר על ידי עצמו,[73] i. e. "the word of the murderer",
נדר אלמנה[74] whence אמרה הריני נזירה לאחר שלשים יום אף על פי שנשאת בתוך שלשים יום אינו יכול להפר,[75] i. e. "the vow of one who is a widow",
קללת אלהים[76] whence שכינה . . . אומרת קלני מראשי . . . אם כן המקום מצטער[77]

"a paining of God";
of the second class:
דבר השמטה[78] whence יאמר . . . משמט אני, i. e. "the word of release",[79]
דבר הרוצח[80] whence יאמר רוצח אני,[81] i. e. "the word of 'murderer' ",
קללת אלהים[82] whence מפני שברך את השם,[83] i. e. "the cursing of God" and שם שמים מתחלל,[84] i. e. "the belittlement of God",
פטר . . . רחם[85] whence עד שיפטרו רחם, i. e. "the opening of the womb",[86]
פטר חמור[87] whence עד שיהא היולד חמור, i. e. "the opening of a donkey;[88]
of the third class:
פטר חמור[89] whence והנולד חמור, i. e. "the opening which is a donkey";[90]
of the fourth class:
ערי הלוים[91] whence עד שיהא לוי ובערי הלויים,[92] i. e. "cities of the Levites",
בגד אלמנה[93] whence אלמנה בין שהיא עניה בין שהיא עשירה אין ממשכנין אותה, i. e. "the dress of a widow;[94]
of the fifth class:
ערי הלוים[95] whence אין הדברים אמורים אלא בערי הלויים[96] i. e. "Levitical cities",
ערות דבר[97] whence דבר ערוה,[98] i. e. "some unseemliness" or[99] על פי שנים עדים, i. e. "substantiated unseemliness".

It was the theory of some of the Tannaitic expositors that the genitive possessed *conjunctive* force, e. g. ערות דבר[100] was thought to be equivalent to ערוה ודבר,[101] and קהל עדת ישראל[102] to קהל ועדה וישראל.[103]

Of the two nouns the one *determined* was considered as containing the main thought according to קן[104] (צפור) = קן מכל מקום,[105] and אל תוך רחובה[106] whence היתה רחובה חוצה לה כונסין אותה לתוכה.[107]

The determination of nouns by others standing in *apposition* to them is noted in the following instances:
in ועשית עולותיך הבשר והדם[108] הבשר והדם stands in apposition to עולותיך,[109]
in ויהי ערב ויהי בקר יום אחד[110] יום אחד stands in apposition to ערב . . . בקר.[111]

There are also instances recorded of the determination of nouns by *prepositional phrases*:

thus in על מוקדה על המזבח[112] על המזבח determines מוקדה,[113]
in פטר כל רחם בבני ישראל[114] בבני ישראל determines[115] פטר,
in כתית למאור[116] למאור determines כתית,[117]
in מכל חטאתיכם לפני ה'[118] לפני ה' determines חטאתיכם,[119]
in אלהיהם על ההרים[120] על ההרים determines אלהיהם,[121]
in כסף וזהב עליהם[122] עליהם determines כסף וזהב.[123]

Prepositional phrases may also be in apposition with each other, in which case the preposition is repeated as in עד מקום שכם עד אלון מורה[124] i. e. שכם = אלון מורה,[125] and על מוקדה על המזבח[126] i. e. מוקדה = מזבח.[127]

From the noun we turn to the *personal pronoun.* The general theory of the Tannaitic Bible expositors, as evidenced in the Mishnah, was that the use of pronouns not absolutely necessary to the sense indicated emphasis. This principle was applied in the following instances:
(וכתב) **לה**[128] = לשמה,[129] i. e. for "her";
(ואשה גרושה) מאישה[130] = ולא מאיש שאינו אישה,[131] i. e. "her" husband;
(על) חטאתו[132] = לשם חטאו (שיהא קרבנו),[133] i. e. "his" sin;
והשבותו[134] = ראה היאך תשיבנו לו,[135] i. e. return "it";
אשר חטא בה[136] = פרט למתעסק,[137] i. e. "that" wherewith he sinned;
(לא ירבה) **לו** (סוסים)[138] = אלא כדי מרכבתו,[139] i. e. for "himself";
(וכסף וזהב לא ירבה) **לו** (מאד)[140] = אלא כדי ליתן אספניא[141] i. e. for "himself";
שללה[142] = ולא שלל השמים[143] i. e., "its" spoil;
(ראשית בכורי) אדמתך[144] = עד שיהו כל הגדולין מאדמתך,[145] i. e. "thy" soil;
(ולא יראה) **לך**[146] = חמץ של עכו"ם שעבר עליו הפסח מותר ושל ישראל אסור,[147] i. e. of "thine".

Particularly, however, did it obtain in the case of the disjunctive personal pronoun where a conjunctive one might have been employed, as in (ואתן) **אתם** (לאהרן)[148] = אין לו אלא מה שאמור בענין,[149] i. e. "them".

A similar function was attributed to unnecessary *numerals* as e. g. in (ומת) אחד (מהם)[150] = שעליה זיקת יבם אחד,[151], i. e. "one", especially if a restrictive personal pronoun was added to the numeral, as in (גם) שניהם[152] = שנים ולא ארבעה . . . הן ולא ולדותיהן i. e. "the two of them".

Numerals occurring singly were recognized as being used in

a distributive sense, as e. g. in ושתים דלתות להיכל ולקדש[154] which was interpreted וד' דלתות היו לו שתים בפנים ושתים בחוץ,[155] i. e. "two each".

Another way of indicating emphasis was seen in the *demonstrative pronouns*.

The particle זה was construed both as a *demonstrative*, as e. g. in בננו זה[156] = זהו שלקה בפניכם,[157] i. e. "this" son of ours,
and in כיום הזה[158] = מה היום הזה הולך ואינו חוזר,[159] i. e. "this" day,
or as a mere *enclitic of place*, as in
בננו זה[160] whence ולא סומין[161] i. e. our son "here",
and כיום הזה[162] = מה היום מאפיל ומאיר,[163] i. e. the day "here".

The *tone* alone was also seen as a means of throwing light on the meaning, as e. g. in כל מנחת כהן כליל תהיה לא תאכל[164] whence priestly expositors were said to have inferred: הואיל ועומר ושתי הלחם ולחם הפנים שלנו היאך נאכלים,[165] i. e. they emphasized כל.

Apropos the Mishnaic exegetes' construction of the use of the *particles* we have already noted previously the two renderings of the *adverb* תמיד.[166]

There are also on record two different interpretations of לא .. עוד[167] in the sense of "never"[168] and in that of "no repetition of the customary".[169]

As for the *prepositions* it has been remarked that
על was known to have the meaning at times of "on" and at others of "near".[170]
עד was construed as "up to and including" e. g. עד עצם היום הזה[171] whence יום הנף כולו אסור,[172] although as has been observed previously it might also have the meaning of "up to but not including".[173]

The ground meaning of עם in the conception of Mishnaic exegesis as "together with" has also been noted already.[174] Whether in a numerical sense as in "והתיצבו שם עמך",[175] it meant "together with and including"[176] or "together with but not including"[177] was a moot point between the exegetes.

Of the uncommon uses of other prepositions the Mishnah notes
אֶל in the sense of "on", as e. g. in וישא . . . את ידו אל העם[178] whence מגביה ידיו למעלה מן הציץ[179];
ב in the sense of "up to" or "adjoining", as e. g. in במספר ארבעים (יכנו)[180] whence מנין שהוא סמוך לארבעים,[181] and in the sense of "by"

(of the agent), which use has been observed above ;[182]
כ in the sense of "something like", as e. g. in כנגע נראה לי[183] whence לא יגזור ויאמר נגע;[184]
ל in the possessive sense of "belonging to" rather than the agent in "לא יראה לך"[185] whence של ישראל אסור[186] i. e. "of that which belongs to thee";
מן in the partitive sense of "belonging to the class", as e. g. in אשר לא משדה אחוזתו[187] whence שאינה ראויה להיות שדה אחוזה, in the time sense of "after", as e.g. in מקץ שבע שנים[189] whence במוצאי שביעית,[190] or the comparative sense, as e.g. in קורא הדרות מראש[191] whence במספר הדורות לפניו[192].

The policy was to construe prepositions simply, not assuming ellipsis of one preposition where two might be detected. Thus כיום הזה[193] is rendered "like this day" (מה היום הזה . . . אף)[194] not "as on this day",[195] and בראשון[196] is interpreted as "on the first (month)" (ניסן),[197] not as "as of yore".[198]

Adverbial ideas were known to be expressed not only by adverbs or prepositional phrases but also by nouns without the preposition. Thus
קרית must be construed as local, i. e. "in", in אריאל קרית חנה דוד[199] because אריאל is interpreted as ההיכל[200]
בית ה' אלהיך used in connection with תביא[201] is twice interpreted as denoting place to which, i. e. "into." In one instance the comment is עד שיביא להר מבית,[202] in the other באה לבית[203]
Time was evidently believed to be implied by בכורי מעשיך in וחג הקציר בכורי מעשיך[204] whence אין מביאין בכורים קודם לעצרת.[205]

A considerable number of interpretations have as their problem the construction of the *conjunctions.* Among these the conjunction ו figures most prominently. As the connecting link between words there were ascribed to it not only conjunctive and alternative, but also explicative and copulative functions. Illustrative of the first are:
זכר ונקבה בראם[206] whence בנים . . . זכר ונקבה,[207] i. e. "male and (also) female",
ויצאו זקניך ושופטיך[208] whence זקניך שנים ושופטיך שנים,[209] i. e. thy elders" and (also)" thy judges.
An extreme case is the interpretation by R Aḳiba of ונטמאה in

אשר תשטה אשה תחת אישה ונטמאה[210] to indicate that כשם שאסורה לבעל כך אסורה לבועל.[211]
Illustrative of the second is:
זכר ונקבה בראם [212] whence בנים . . . שני זכרים, i. e. male "or"[213] female.
Illustrative of the third is:
ויצאו זקניך ושופטיך[214] whence זקניך שנים . . . שלשה מבית דין הגדול,[215] i. e. "thy elders, namely thy judges".[216]
Illustrative of the fourth are:
בחריש ובקציר[217] which indicates that מה חריש רשות אף קציר רשות,[218]
אישה יקימנו ואישה יפירנו[219] which indicates that את שבא לכלל הקם בא לכלל הפר,[220] והיה הוא ותמורתו יהיה קדש[221] which indicates that היכן קדושה חלה עליו בבית בעלים אף תמורה בבית בעלים[222] and מה הוא מיוחד אף תמורתו מיוחדת.[223]

In a *series* in which this conjunction is used its omission before any but the last word was evidently considered allowable, for וזבחת פסח . . . צאן ובקר[224] serves להקיש כל הבא מן הבקר והצאן לפסח.[225]

In the use of this conjunction as a *connective* of clauses various functions have been distinguished. Besides serving to connect coordinate clauses it could also introduce subordinate clauses denoting purpose or result, clauses taking the place of nouns or the apodoses of conditions.
Illustrations of the first are:
(ולא ירבה לו נשים) ולא יסור לבבו[226] whence אפילו אחת ומסירה את לבו הרי זה לא ישאנה,[227] i. e. "and" his heart should not turn aside,
(או נפש אשר תגע . . . בנבלת שרץ טמא) ונעלם ממנו[228] whence על העלם שרץ חייב,[229] i. e. "and" it be hidden from him, and
(ופנו את הבית) . . . ולא יטמא (כל אשר בבית)[230] whence ואפילו חבילי עצים[231] (that are not susceptible to contamination), i. e. "and" there shall not become contaminated.
Illustrations of the second are:
(ופנו את הבית) . . . ולא יטמא (כל אשר בבית)[232] upon the interpretation of which by R Judah R Simon remarked עסק הוא לפנוי,[233] i. e. "in order" that there may not be contaminated, and
(עד דרוש אחיך אותו) והשבותו (לו)[234] whence ראה היאך תשיבנו לו,[235] i. e. "in order" that thou mayest return it.
Illustrations of the third are:
ולא ירבה לו נשים ולא יסור לבבו[236] whence מרבה הוא לו ובלבד שלא יהו

מסירות את לבו,[237] i. e. he shall not take "so" many "that" his heart will turn, and

ויעתר לו.. וישיבהו . . למלכותו[238] whence למלכותו השיבו ולא לחיי העו"הב,[239] i. e. and He listened to him . . ."so that" He restored him to his kingdom.

Illustrative of the fourth is:

ונעלם ממנו והוא טמא[240] whence על העלם טומאה חייב[241] i. e. and it be hidden from him "that" he is unclean.

Illustrative of the fifth are:

(ונתן האיש) . . . ולו תהיה לאשה[242] whence אינה ראויה לבא בישראל אינו רשאי לקיימה,[243] i. e. "if" she be a wife (suited to him),

והלך לפניך צדקך כבוד ה' יאספך[244] whence ולא על משה לבד אמרו (that God buried him) אלא על כל הצדיקים,[245] i. e. "if" thy righteousness go before thee, then . . . and

ונקלה אחיך לעיניך[246] whence כשלקה הרי הוא כאחיך,[247] i. e. if he has been humbled, he is a brother in thy eyes.

Another conjunction the various functions of which seem to have been noticed by the Tannaitic expositors is כי. We find it construed as *temporal*, as e. g. in

כי תבצר . . . לא תעולל[248] whence אין לעניים בעוללות קודם לבציר[249] i. e. "when" thou takest in the vintage;

or as *conditional*, as e. g. in

כי תבצר . . (לא תעולל)[250] whence אם אין בציר מניין עוללות,[251] i. e. "if" thou takest in the vintage;

also as *causal* as e. g. in

והיה אם לא תמצא חן . . . כי מצא (בה ערות דבר)[252] whence אלא אם כן מצא בה דבר ערוה[253] and

אפילו הקדיחה תבשילו,[254] i. e. "because" he found;

or as *illustrative*, as e. g. in

(והיה אם לא תמצא חן) . . כי מצא בה[255] whence אפילו מצא אחרת נאה הימנה[256] i. e. "as for example" if he has found in her . . .

The conjunction אם introducing the apodosis of a conditional sentence is commented on but once in connection with אם לא שלח ידו[257] whence it it deduced that אינו חייב עד שישלח[258] i. e. "if".

The *comparative* force of אשר is recognized in ואשר יבא את רעהו[259] whence מה יער רשות . . . ליכנס שם יצא חצר בעל הבית[260] i. e. "as when".

A *corrective* or explicative value must have been attributed at times to the alternative conjunction או as in אם יום או יומים יעמד[261] whence יום יומים (מעת לעת) = יום או יומים,[262] i. e. "or rather".

Correlative comparative particles were probably recognized in . . כ . . כ in איש כמתנת ידו כברכת ה' אלהיך[263] which was applied to one who had מרובים (נכסים) וזה (אוכלין) וזה[264] i. e. "like" the gift of his hand "like" the blessing of God.

Finally it appears that the subordination of one clause to another by *asyndeton* was also recognized as possible. This is implied in the citation of the verse עת לעשות לה', הפרו תורתך[265] of which one part is obviously made subordinate to the other.[266]

IV

Critical Observations on the Bible in Mishnaic Exegesis.

The aforegoing two chapters have been confined to the treatment in the exegesis of the Mishnah of individual words or constructions. It is fitting now that we regard the broader critical aspects of Mishnaic Bible interpretation. With the background of the Tannaitic expositors, with their historical and text-critical theories we have already become somewhat familiarized. But that is only in a general way. The details still have to be examined, and our picture of Mishnaic exegesis cannot be complete without such an examination.

The data that are to be found in the Mishnah under the heading of criticism are quite variegated in character and form a category by themselves. They range all the way from reflections on accentuation and verse division and other phenomena of the text to the determination of time and the identification of obscure allusions. That the massoretic punctuation is not always followed in the Bible exegesis of the Mishnah has been previously asserted and is to be elaborated here. We note the following two instances of deviation from the massoretic verse division:

והכהו לפניו כדי רשעתו במספר. ארבעים יכנו (Dt XXV 2.3) is by one expositor divided והכהו לפניו כדי רשעתו. במספר ארבעים יכנו,[1] and

תמימים יהיו לכם. ומנחתם סלת בלולה (Num XXVIII 19.20) is read as if the punctuation were תמימים יהיו לכם ומנחתם.[2]

Examples of punctuation within the verse different from the massoretic are:

(Jos VIII 33) נגד–הכהנים, הלוים[3] instead of נגד הכהנים–הלוים,

(Ex XXIII 2) לנטת, אחרי רבים–להטות[4] instead of לנטת–אחרי רבים, להטת,

(Dt XXV 3) ונקלה, אחיך–לעיניך[5] instead of ונקלה–אחיך לעיניך,

(Lev XXVII 28) כל חרם–קדש קדשים, הוא לה'[6] instead of כל חרם קדש (קדשים)-הוא לה'.

(Lev XXVII 21) כשדה (החרם)–לכהן[7] instead of כשדה–החרם, לכהן

There is one case also where ellipsis seems to have been assumed, the word being read with both what precedes and what follows. That is Dt XXV 9 וענתה ואמרה→ככה←יעשה לאיש according to one authority.[8]

Conjunctions and prepositions were by some taken to connect with the *nearest* noun or verb modifiable, e. g.

in תמימים יהיו לכם ונסכיהם (Num XXVIII 31) in which נסכיהם is joined to the subject implied in יהיו,[9]

in ועשרון סולת אחד בלול בשמן למנחה ולוג שמן (Lev XIV 21) where לוג שמן is coordinate with מנחה,[10] and

in והנותר . . . יתן . . . לכפר (Lev XIV 29)[11] where לכפר modifies יתן.

So also in והאריאל שתים עשרה ארך בשתים עשרה רחב רבוע אל ארבעת רבעיו (Ez XLIII 16) the apposite רבוע was taken to stand in apposition not to אריאל but to the entire clause,[14]

or what is *further* away, as

in ועשרון סולת . . . למנחה ולוג שמן (Lev XIV 21)[12] where לוג שמן is coordinate with עשרון, and

in והנותר . . . יתן . . . לכפר (Lev XIV 29)[13] where לכפר refers to what precedes.

All indications lead to the conclusion that the text of Scripture was thoroughly mastered and carefully scrutinized by the Tannaitic expositors. Not only were contradictions, repetition and redundancies noted and explained as has already been remarked above.[15] Attention was paid even to massoretic points, words were counted and their relative position commented on. Thus for example R Jose deduces from the fact that there is a

point over the ה of רחוקה[16] (Num IX 10) that that word is not to be taken in its strict sense.
The importance of the covenant of circumcision is inferred from the occurrence of the term ברית thirteen times in Gen XVII[17] and also from the fact that the epithet תמים[18] is first there applied to Abraham.[19]
A lesson is derived from the fact that in Ex V 2 the name of Pharaoh occurs before the tetragrammaton whereas in Ex IX 27 the latter comes before the former's reference to himself.[20]
The question of the chronological order of the operations mentioned played a part in the interpretation of ... ואחר ישקה Num V 26[21] the meaning of which is not quite clear on account of the occurrence of the expression והשקה in verses 24 and 27.[22]

It was not only the external features of the text that were exploited. The deeper implications, too, were turned to account. Concerning the strict or loose interpretation of scriptural passages, the inference from a statement regarding the contrary and the significance of superflous synonyms we have spoken previously.[23] These were however, not the only means of bringing to light the hidden meanings of Scripture resorted to. Sometimes a biblical statement implies certain obvious assumptions. These assumptions were brought out. For example
from והשיבו אותו אל עיר מקלטו (Num XXXV 25) it was deduced that the murderer had gone to the city of refuge before being tried;[24]
from ועשיתם לו כאשר זמם לעשות לאחיו (Dt XIX 19) that the falsely accused has not yet been executed;[25]
from ואל פתח אהל מועד לא הביאו ... דם יחשב לאיש ההוא (Lev XVII 4) that only those sacrifices that are supposed to be offered up within the sanctuary precincts are referred to;[26]
from והשמותי את מקדשיכם (Lev XXVI 31) that holy places retain their sacred character even when they are in ruins;[27]
from the contrast of the scoffers with those who delight in the Torah (Psalms I 1.2) that whoever does not study Torah must be a scoffer;[28]
from the prefacing of negative commandments by the statement אשר יעשה אתם האדם וחי בהם (Lev XVIII 5)[29] that desisting from what is forbidden is equivalent to doing positive good.

Significance was seen in the correspondence by numbers or other similarities of certain events in the lives of biblical characters, for example
Samson's going after the sight of his eyes and his loss of his eyesight at the hands of the Philistines,[30]
Absalom's vanity over his hair and his being hung by his hair,[31]
his rape of the ten concubines of his father and his assassination by means of ten lances by the armor-bearers of Joab,[32]
his deceiving of three hearts[33] and the thrusting of three darts into his heart,[34]
Miriam's waiting for Moses[35] and Israel's waiting for her,[36]
Josef's burial of Jacob,[37] the transportation of his own earthly remains by Moses[38] and the latter's burial by God.[39]

Incidental remarks in the non-legal portions of the Bible were considered as clues regarding popular usage or regarding the nature of things. Thus
from Is XXX 14 it was concluded that potsherds were employed in taking out fire or drawing water and that pieces smaller than those required for such purposes were of no value,[40]
from Ex XIX 15 that three days separation is required for complete sexual purification,
from Gen XXXIV 25 that the third day after the circumcision is that of[41] greatest pain,[42]
from Ps CIX 18 that oil is as soothing to the bones as water is to the thirst,[43]
from I Sam XII 17 that rain during the wheat harvest is a calamity,[44]
from Amos IV 7 that for a city to suffer drought whilest others have rain is unnatural,[45]
from Lev XXIV 14 that the stoning place was outside the court.[46]

Further characteristics of the Bible criticism of the Mishnah are
the *removal of anthropomorphisms* (as e. g. that inherent in Dt XX 4 in which either ה' אלהיכם or ההלך עמכם are interpreted figuratively,[47])
metaphorization (as e. g. Ex XVII 11[48] Num XXI 8[49] and Dt XXI 7,[50])

allegorization, (as of[51] Cant III 11) and
the *elaboration* on texts not sufficiently explicit (like Lev XXII 13,[52] Dt XXV 8,[53] Num V 17,[54] Jos VIII 33,[55] Dt XXIV 5,[56] Ex XXII 13.14,[57] Dt XVII 16.17.19,[58] Dt XVII 7,[59] Zech VI 14,[60] Ez XLI 24.[61])
There are only a few instances in Mishnaic Bible exegesis of metaphors being taken literally such as
יעור in Ex XXIII 8 which is interpreted as actually "blinding"[62] and
Is I 18[63] whence it is deduced that a crimson colored-strap put on the head of the sin-offering turns white.
On the other hand from the statement (Soṭ IX 9) with reference to Micah VII 1 משמת יוסי . . . בטלו האשכולות it is clear that אשכול was recognized as a[64] metaphor for its parallel חסיד which is mentioned in verse 2.

Interesting are the observations explicit or implied in Mishnaic exegesis regarding time and person speaking, addressed or referred to of scriptural passages.
Under the heading of the first group may be classed
the discussion as to whether the event predicted in Jer XLIX 6 has already been fulfilled,
the admission that the prophecy of Amos IX 14 has not,[65]
the assignment of Is XXV 8 to the distant future[66] and
the application of the description of the temple in Ez XLVI 21.22 to the ideal temple of the future.[67]
As to the second a distinction must be made between proverbs introduced by the formulae על זה נאמר, עליך הוא אומר or עליהם נאמר, which are only loosely applied, and actual identification.
The former includes Pr XXII 28,[68] Pr XXIII 25,[69] Eccl I 15,[70] Eccl IV 12,[71] I Sam II 6,[72] Ps L 5,[73] Lev XIX 16 and Pr XI 13.[74]
Under the latter we group the following intimations:
מחוקק Dt XXXIII 21 = Moses.[75]
עדה Num XIV 27 = the ten spies.[76]
אדם Gen VI 3 = the generation of the flood.[77]
רשעים Ps I 5 = the generation of the flood.[78]
חטאים Ps I 5 = the inhabitants of Sodom.[79]
נשיא Lev IV 22 = the king.[80]

Ex XXIII 2 is addressed to judges.[81]
Of Dt XXI 8 "כפר . . . ישראל" is recited by the priests while "ונכפר להם הדם" is uttered by the Holy Spirit.[82]
The logical subject of ונקרא Dt XXV 10 are the זקנים of verse 9.[83]
By לנו Dt XXVI 15 are meant all Jews whose ancestors have received a share in Palestine.[84]
By לכם Pr IV 2 are meant the Jews.[85]
By לי Ex XIII 8 is meant the individual Jew.[86]
By אליך Ex XX 24 is meant the individual.[87]
In Lev XIV 42 the plurals refer to the two neighbors, the singular to the owner of the afflicted house.[88]
Is XXIV 9,[89] used as a description of conditions that obtained since the Synhedrin was abolished, and Ps XII 2[90] of those existing since the destruction of the Temple, were probably meant to be loosely applied.
The terms תלמידיו של אברהם אבינו and תלמידיו של בלעם הרשע applied to אהבי Pr VIII 21 and אנשי דמים ומרמה Ps LV 24 respectively[91] did not apply to specific individuals but are general names for lovers of God and wicked men.

Among the curios of Mishnaic Bible exegesis must finally be mentioned the implications recognized in the numerical value of the letters of a word of which there is the following example: יש (Pr VIII 21) = 310.[92]

V

Exegetical Methods Employed in Mishnaic Bible Interpretation

We have had an opportunity to obtain an insight into the materials of Mishnaic Bible exegesis and it remains for us now to inquire into the means whereby the Tannaitic expositors arrived at their conclusions, how they established the meaning of a term, the correct construction of a word, phrase or clause and the underlying significance, the deeper implications of the scriptural text. For the solution of this problem the disclosures of the Mishnah itself are not sufficient. It is necessary to go beyond to kindred collections of Tannaitic lore where the exegesis of passages, briefly commented on in the Mishnah, is given more in extenso and the process of the hermeneutics more perspicacious.

Some of the exegetical methods of the Mishnaic expositors of the Bible which, for want of a better name, might be called auxiliaries have already been mentioned before. It has been noted that the Tannaitic exegetes were assisted in their Bible interpretation by traditions regarding the meaning of words and popular usage, as well as by their knowledge of the neo-Hebrew and Aramaic languages, which were current in their milieu. These means it seems, however, were insufficient for the elicitation of the full sense of the biblical texts. They had to be supplemented by methods of a more independent character. One of these methods was *etymology*. The following vocables of the Bible are elucidated by indications of their ground meaning or origin:
אריאל,[1] בליעל,[2] גבן,[3] ידון,[4] מאדך,[5] מורה,[6] מרוח אשך,[7] נקלה[8] and שעטנז.[9]

Another means to which the Mishnaic exegetes resorted in order to clear up obscurities of meaning or syntax was that of *equating* the corresponding members of parallel portions of a verse. Clear examples of such equations in the Mishnah are:
Ps I 5 בעדת צדיקים || במשפט[10]
Jos VI 5 שופר || קרן[11]
II Sam I 20 ערלים || פלשתים[12]
Ps XL 3 יון || בור[13]

Among these parallels indicating synonymity of meaning or equivalence of construction may also be included
Dt XIII 17 לא תבנה עוד || והיתה תל עולם[14]
Is XXX 22 צא תאמר לו || תזרם[15]
Ex XXIII 16 בצאת השנה (חג האסיף) || בכורי מעשיך (חג הקציר)[16]
Ps XXV 14 להודיעם || סוד[17]
Gen I 10 ימים || ארץ[18]
Dt VI 7 ובשכבך ובקומך || ובלכתך בדרך[19]

Allied means of identification were *apposition*:

e. g. Gen XII 6 עד מקום שכם, עד אלון מורה,[20] therefore אלון מורה = שכם;
Gen I 5 ערב . . . בקר, יום אחד,[21] therefore ערב ובקר = יום אחד;
I Sam XVII 36 הפלשתי, הערל,[22] therefore פלשתי = ערל;

and Dt VII 27 עלתיך, הבשר והדם,[23] therefore עלתיך = הבשר והדם;
to which may be added Dt XXII 6 (קן) צפר . . . אפרוחים או ביצים;[24]
predication:
e. g. Jer IX 25 כל הגוים(=)ערלים;[25] also ולמקוה מים (קרא) ימים[26]
causal explanation:
e. g. Jud XIII 5 מורה לא יעלה על ראשו, כי נזיר אלהים יהיה הנער,[27]
hence מורה has something to do with נזיר;
Dt XXIV 6 לא יחבל רחים ורכב, כי נפש הוא חובל,[28] hence רחים ורכב = נפש.
and *genitive determination*:
e. g. Lev XIX 9 לקט קצירך,[79] hence איזהו לקט הנושר בשעת הקצירה;
Lev XIX 10 פרט כרמך,[30] hence איזהו פרט הנושר בשעת הבצירה.

There were also recognized other ways whereby the correct meaning of a term could be inferred from the context itself. One was *contrast*:
e. g. in בקר וצאן (Lev XXVII 32) צאן is contrasted with בקר and therefore signifies not sheep but Kleinvieh.
Another was *elimination*:
e. g. in the verse ונאכל גדיש או הקמה או השדה (Ex XXII 5), since all that grows on the field is mentioned and השדה is the alternative, השדה can only refer to the soil;[32]
in האשם המושב לה' לכהן מלבד איל הכפורים (Num V 8) אשם cannot refer to the guilt-offering which is indicated by איל הכפורים and must, therefore, refer to the monetary compensation owed.[33]
A third was *logical incompatibility*: e. g.
על in ועליו מטה מנשה Num II 20 cannot possibly mean "on", but must be construed "near",[34];
למת in ולא נתתי ממנו למת Dt XXVI 14 cannot mean 'give "to" the dead', because to the dead nothing is given, and must therefore be interpreted "for" the dead.[35]

Finally the verse as a whole could intimate approximately the significance of an expression. It is e. g. evident from ולמדנה בנותיכם נהי ואשה רעותה קינה (Jer IX 19) that קינה is a sort of antiphonic lament.[36]

To these simple means of exposition by internal evidence must be added Rabbi Ishmael's copulative interpretation of the ו[37] and the theory of סמוכין which have been dealt with previously.[38]

If the meaning of the reading in a certain verse is not clear, light can be thrown on it by the *adjacent* verse. The expression used for such illumination was חברו מוכיח עליו.[39] Instances in which this method was unmistakeably applied in the Mishnah are

the reading in Cant I 2 is דּוֹדֶיךָ as indicated by על כן עלמות אהבוך verse 3;[40]

גדי in Dt XIV 21 refers only to the young of animals whose carcass is prohibited as proven by לא תאכלו כל נבלה at the beginning of the verse;[41]

פרו ורבו in Gen I 28 are addressed to the זכר ונקבה in the verse previous;[42]

מבן ששים שנה ומעלה in Lev XXVII 7 clarifies the age indications in the preceding verses;[43]

similarly בתי ערי הלוים (Lev XXV 33) refers to houses owned by Levites in the Levitical cities as proven by ואשר יגאל מן הלוים in the preceding verse;[44]

מושב לצים (Ps I 1) is a session of those who do not engage in the study of the Torah as indicated by the contrast in verse 2;[45]

לא יבא . . . בקהל ה' (Dt XXIII 2) refers to having marital relations[46] in keeping with the preceding verse;

לא תהיה אחרי רבים לרעת (Ex XXIII 2) ostensibly has reference to the conduct of judges in the court room as the sequel shows; ולא תביא תועבה אל ביתך (Dt VII 26) is interpreted as a prohibition against the bringing of idols into the house[48] no doubt because of the injunction in the verse preceding where פסילי אלהיהם are designated תועבת ה' אלהיך.

Of the practice of the Mishnaic Bible expositors of ascertaining the meaning of a word in one context from its use in another where it is less obscure we have already spoken once before.[49] In the language of the Tannaim this sort of analogy is called גזרה שוה.[50] Explicit cases in the Mishnah are:

דבר Dt XXIV 1 = דבר Dt XIX 15[51]
ענה Dt XXVI 5 = ענה Dt XXVII 14[52]
ענה Dt XXV 9 = ענה Dt XXVII 14[53]
אלני מרה Dt XI 30 = אלון מורה Gen XII 6[54]
עדה Num XXXV 24, 25 = עדה Num XIV 27[55] and Lev IV 13
על Lev XXIV 27 = על Num II 20[56]

יום אחד Lev XXII 28 = יום אחד Gen I 5[57]
מורה I Sam I 11 = מורה Jud XIII 5[58]
זולל וסבא Dt XXI 20 = זולל וסבא Pr XXIII 20[59]
צאן Dt XVIII 4 = צאן Is VII 21[60]
or צאן I Sam XXV 18[61]
שוב שבות Jer XLIX 6 = שוב שבות Amos IX 14[62]

The formula employed in most of these cases is נאמר כאן . . . ונאמר להלן . . . מה להלן . . אף כאן . . .[63]

Proven from the other Tannaitic sources as having been determined by means of גזרה שוה are:

אבד Num XVI 33[64] = אבד Ps CXIX 176[65]
איתן Dt XXI 4[66] = איתן Num XXIV 21,[67] Micah VI 2[68] and Jer V 15[69]
התעמר Dt XXIV 7[70] = התעמר Dt XXI 14[71]
רע Lev XXVII 10[72] = רע Dt XVII 1[73]
יהיה Dt XXIV 5[74] = יהיה Lev XIX 24[75]
ירא אלהים Job I 1[76] = ירא אלהים Gen XXII 12[77]
דרך רחוקה Num IX 10[78] = דרך רחוקה Dt XIV 24[79]
אתנן זונה Dt XXIII 19[80] = אתנן זונה[81] Ex XVI 33
מחיר Dt XXIII 19[82] = מחיר Ps XLIV 13[83]

Supplied with analogies by the Talmudim are:

בא ב Dt XXIII 2[84] = בא ב I Kings XI 2[85]
דִּבֵּר Dt XX 2[86] = דִּבֵּר Ex XIX 19[87]
ולו תהיה לאשה Dt XXII 29[88] = ולו תהיה לאשה Dt XXII 19.[89]

Further examples of the use of this method of elucidation are probably furnished by the following:

דוה Is XXX 22[90] = נדה as in Lev XII 2
ראשון Joel II 23[91] = החודש הראשון as in Gen VIII 13
בריתי Jer XXXIII 25[92] = ברית מילה as in Gen XVII 2
אלהים Ps LXXXII 1[93] = judges as in Ex XXII 7 ff
תורתי Pr IV 2[94] = Torah as in Dt XXXI 11
המזבח אשר לפני ה׳ Lev XVI 18[95] = מזבח הזהב as in Lev IV 7
מקץ Dt XXXI 10[96] = "after the end" as in Gen XLI 1
מועד Dt XXXI 10[97] = "festival" as in Lev XXIII 2
כליל Dt XIII 17[98] = עולה as in Lev XXIII 2
חטאים Ps I 5[99] = אנשי סדום as in Gen XIII 13
כורתי בריתי עלי זבח Ps L 5[100] = דור המדבר as in Ex XXIV 6 and 8.

As we have learned before, contraditions within Scripture were inadmissible according to the Bible exegetes of the Mishnah.[101] To interpret apparently contradictory passages in such a manner that they did not conflict became therefore another rule of exegesis for them.

One means of harmonization was to make the conflicting utterances apply to different matters. This is done in the following instances or situations:

Lev V 19a אשם הוא vs b אשם אשם לה׳[102]

Num XXXV 4 אלף אמה vs 5 אלפים באמה[103]

Ex XXIII 2a לא תהיה אחרי רבים לרעת vs c אחרי רבים להטת[104]

Gen XV 13 וענו אתם ארבע מאות שנה vs 16 ודור רביעי ישובו הנה[105]

Lev I 9 והקטיר הכהן את הכל המזבחה vs Dt XII 27 ועשית עלתיך הבשר והדם[106]

Lev XXVII 22 כשדה החרם לכהן תהיה אחוזתו vs 28 כל חרם קדש קדשים הוא לה׳[107]

Lev XXVII 26 אך בכור ... לא יקדיש vs Dt XV 19 כל הבכור ... תקדיש.[108]

Another means of reconciliation was so to expound one of the conflicting passages as to make it agree with the other. This is done in the case of:

Dt XXIV 21 כי תבצר כרמך ... לא תעולל in favor of Lev XIX 10[109] וכרמך לא תעולל

Dt XVI 2 וזבחת פסח לה׳ אלהיך צאן ובקר in favor of Ex XII 5[110] מן הכבשים ומן העזים תקחו

Dt XIX 21 נפש בנפש in favor of 19[111] ועשיתם לו כאשר זמם

Ex XXI 21a אך אם יום in favor of b[112] יומים

Dt XXV 2 במספר in favor of 3[113] ארבעים יכנו

Dt XX 9c בפניו in favor of a[114] לעיני הזקנים.

A third method of dealing with contradictory passages was to give one preference over the other. While there is no explicit illustration of this method in the Mishnah there are interpretations found in it which, as confirmed from other sources, are the result of such exegesis, e. g.:

Ex XXII 7 אם לא שלח ידו over against 8 על כל דבר פשע[115]

Dt XXIV 7 והתעמר בו ומכרו over against Ex XXI 17[116] ונמצא בידו

Lev VII 33 המקריב over against Lev VII 14 לכהן הזרק[117]

Num IX 13 דרך over against 10 דרך רחוקה[118]

Num V 26 ואחר ישקה over against 24 והשקה.[119]

Since contradiction within Scripture was precluded, interpretations that would lead to contradiction had to be avoided. Thus מורה in I Sam I 11 ומורה לא יעלה על ראשו could not be "fear" because as I Sam XVI 2 indicates כבר היה עליו מורא של בשר ודם.[120]
Num XIV 35 ושם ימותו could not mean אין עומדין בדין because of Ps L 5.[121]
Similarly the reason why b Zoma did not interpret Dt XVI 3[122] to apply to the era of the Messiah was due to Jer XVI 14, 15; and
לא Job XIII 15[124] could not be definitely interpreted as the particle of negation by its spelling because of Is LXIII 9 בכל צרתם לא צר.[125]

Repetition and redundancy were, as has already been noted previously, further guides to exegesis indicating emphasis or extension of application.[126]

Likewise any peculiarity of expression or construction was the occasion for the display of the ingenuity of the expositor. Thus, for example,
the use of the preposition מן in אשר לא משדה אחוזתו Lev XXVII 22 is responsible for the interpretation שדה הראויה להיות שדה אחוזה,[127]
of שמע instead of ראה in וכל העם ישמעו ויראו Dt XVII 13 for the opinion that personal presence is not necessary,[128]
the change from the plural to the singular in Lev XIV 42 for the idea that while the transportation of the material is done by both neighbors the plastering is carried out by the owner alone,[129]
the order of the words במספר ארבעים Dt XXV 2, 3 instead of ארבעים במספר for the interpretation of מספר הסמוך לארבעים.[130]

As unusual, and therefore containing implications were also recognized
the use in עזב תעזב עמו Ex XXIII 5 of עמו[131] instead, probably, of לו as in the first part of the verse,
the expression יעשה בזדון Dt XVII 12[132] instead, probably, of יזיד as in Dt XVIII 20,[133]
the form לעושה בשגגה Num V 29[134] instead, probably, of לשוגג as in the previous verse,

the singular יהיה in והיה הוא ותמורתו יהיה Lev XXVII 10[135] instead, probably, of יהיו,[136]
the form זרועיה Is LXI 11[137] for the more usual זרעה.[138]

Finally it was from the careful scrutiny of the Bible as a whole that disclosures as to the correct interpretation of an expression or a passage were derived. Thus
עד in Num V 13 stands for two witnesses[139] because where "one" is meant it is indicated by the word אחד as in Dt XIX 15;[140]
גדי in Dt XIV 21 stands for the young of any domestic mammal[141] because where "kid" is meant the expression גדי עזים is used as in Gen XXXVIII 20.[142]
The interpretation of ונקלה אחיך Dt XXV 3 as כשלקה הרי הוא כאחיך is based on the fact that in the preceding the culprit is referred to only as רשע.[144]
The designation of כהנים as לוים is unusual.[145] Hence the interpretation of Jos VIII 33 ונגד–הכהנים, הלוים.[146]
עדה in עד מתי לעדה הרעה הזאת Num XIV 27 is identified as the spies,[147] no doubt because they are the ones who caused the murmuring מלינים as in verse 36.
כפר לעמך Dt XXI 8 was recited by the כהנים[148] mentioned in verse 5, no doubt because they were the ones who performed the atonement rights, as in Lev XVI 6.
מחוקק Dt XXXIII 21 could be none other than Moses.[149]
רשעים Ps I 5 were identified as the generation of the flood,[150] no doubt because of Gen VI 5.
That II Sam III 31 might not have been the regular procedure is proven from verse 37.[152]
The figurative interpretation of Dt XX 4[153] is supported by I Sam IV 8.[154]
For the construction of Num XXXIII 29, 30, as normative there are arguments pro and con.[155]
The same holds true for the interpretation of מאומה in Dt XIII 18,[156] and of the question as to whether Is II 4 indicates that the wearing of arms is reprehensible or not.[157]

VI

Mishnaic Bible Exegesis in the Light of Modern Criticism

We have tried in the foregoing pages to lay bare the foundations of Mishnaic Bible exegesis, with a view of discovering its true nature, and to give as objective a presentation of our findings as possible. The results that have been obtained warrant the conclusion that, despite the limitations in the light of the standards that obtain today under which they labored, the Tannaitic Bible expositors were by no means the quibblers or casuists they have often been said to be, but that, on the contrary, their interpretation of the Bible, as reflected in the Mishnah at least, was on the whole sober and sane and most of it could stand the test of modern criticism.

Their methods of elucidation were, if we discount those that were due to their hypothesis of the unity of Scripture,[1] essentially those of present day philologians and Bible interpreters.[2] Their syntactical observations indicate a thorough familiarity with the grammar of the Hebrew language which the absence of a scientific terminology like ours did not obscure.[3] Their theory of roots while it was superseded by the classical system of triliteralism is being reconsidered again.[4] At all events the affinity between roots having the strong radicals in common is undoubted.[5]

Their etymology is on the whole quite sound.[6] The one exception pertains to a word of foreign origin,[7] the actual derivation of which has not yet been discovered.[8] The meanings they have given of unusual words are generally correct and have been corroborated by kindred languages.

E. g. מאד[9] = ממון[10] like the Assyrian ma'adu.[11]
שחין[12] = לקה בעץ . . . כל שאינו מחמת האש[13] like Arabic سخن[14]
חרום[15] = הכוחל שתי עיניו כאחת[16] has the same meaning in Arabic (اخرم)[17]

If they attribute to an expression an apparently unnatural significance it is often found, on further examination, that the construction is unusual or the term employed not the common one. Thus:

אחר[18] which is interpreted as "change the order"[19] never occurs without ל governing the infinitive construct except in this instance where it is construed with a direct object;

הכין[20] which is interpreted "make corresponding"[21] is never employed as here with a direct object but always with a phrase introduced by the preposition ל;

מדי חדש בחדשו ומדי שבת בשבתו[22] which is rendered "whenever the month falls on its month etc."[23] is the only instance in which the repeated noun used with the particle מדי has a pronominal suffix.

That עם (עזב תעזב עמו)[24] which is interpreted "with"[25] is not the preposition regularly employed with the logical object of עזב is proven from the first part of the verse.[26]

The use of ב for תחת in נפש בנפש[27] which is rendered "life[28] for life condemned" is uncommon.[29]

לך in ולא יראה לך[30] is construed possessively[31] probably because if an ethical dative were intended בך would have been employed as in Dt XXIII 15.

רגלים[32] as a designation for the pilgrimage festivals[33] is unique. The term regularly used is פעמים.[34]

זרועיה[35] which is taken to contain indications with reference to garden planning[36] is a form that occurs but once.

Their strict interpretation of legal portions of the Pentateuch[37] cannot be found fault with. That is the only way to construe a legal document, nor is there anything unnatural about their theory that repetition or redundancy has the effect of emphasis and extension of application.[38] Their practice of seeking light on the usage and nature of things in the incidental remarks of the books of Sacred Writ is critically sound.[39] Nor is aught amiss with their seeing in the conduct of the heroes of the Bible models to follow or in divining connections between the events of their lives and deriving morals therefrom.[41]

If the sense of certain verses seems to be completely disturbed in order to fit their application, we must be sure whether the interpretation was intended to be actual or whether the passage in question was only loosely applied. That some were only thus employed is proven beyond the shadow of a doubt by definite stereotyped formulae such as על זה נאמר.[42] It is also certain that certain apparent emendations or distortions were meant only as mnemonic devices.[43]

While there are some anachronisms, such as the one that Abraham fulfilled the Torah,[44] that the high-priest Joyada interpreted the Bible in the rabbinic manner,[45] and that Boaz legisated,[46] due to ignorance of historical development, there were on the other hand plausible interpretations of time and person.[47]

Only twice in the Mishnah is a metaphor literally construed.[48] Over against that there are instances in which figures of speech are recognized as such, as for example that אשכול in Micah VII 1 stands for חסיד, as indicated in verse 2,[49]and that Dt XXI 7 is meant in a secondary sense.[50]

The upshot of all these considerations is that the exegesis of the Bible in the Mishnah deserves to be taken more seriously, not merely on account of its interest for the history of Bible exegesis but also as a valuable aid in the correct and critical understanding of Scripture today.

VII

APENDIX

Translations of Biblical Passages in the Light of Mishnaic Exegesis

1. Gen I 5 ויהי ערב ויהי בקר יום אחד and it was evening and it was morning, (i. e.) one day (Ḥull V 5)
2. Gen I 10 ימים (many) seas (Parah VIII 8 || Miḳw V 4 R Meir)
3. Gen I 10 ימים (a) Sea (Parah VIII 8 || Miḳw V 4 R Judah)
4. Gen I 28 ויברך אתם אלהים ויאמר להם אלהים פרו ורבו . . . and God blessed them (m. and f.) and God said to them: "Be fruitful and multiply . ." (Yab VI 6 R Joḥanan b Baroḳa)
5. Gen I 28 ויברך אתם אלהים ויאמר להם אלהים פרו ורבו . . . and God blessed them (m.) and God said to them: "Be fruitful and multiply . . " (Yab VI 6 anon.)
6. Gen IV 10 דמי the bloods (Snh IV 5)
7. Gen IV 10 דמי the portions of the blood (Snh IV 5 other interpretation)
8. Gen V 2 זכר ונקבה בראם male or female he created them (Yab VI 6 Shammaiites)
9. Gen V 2 זכר ונקבה בראם male and female he created them (Yab VI 6 Hillelites)
10. Gen VI 3 לא ידון רוחי באדם לעלם My spirit[a] in man[b] shall not be judged[c] in the world everlasting.[d] (Snh X 3)
11. Gen XII 6 עד מקום שכם עד אלון מורה up to the place of Shekhem, (i. e.) up to Elon More (Soṭ VII 5)
12. Gen XXVI 5 תורתי my Torahs (Kidd IV 14)
13. Gen XXXIV 25 בהיותם כאבים when they were in pain (on account of the circumcision) (Sabb IX 3)
14. Gen XXXIV 25 בהיותם כאבים when they (the members of their bodies) were paining (Sabb XIX 3 R Elazar b Azariah)
15. Ex XII 6 ושחטו אתו כל קהל עדת ישראל and the whole community, even the congregation, even Israel shall slaughter it (Pes V 5)
16. Ex XIII 2 קדש לי כל בכור פטר כל רחם בבני ישראל consecrate unto me every first born—the opening of every womb—among the children of Israel (Bekh VIII 1 anon.)
17. Ex XIII 2 קדש לי כל בכור פטר כל רחם בבני ישראל consecrate unto me every first born, that opens[a] any womb among[b] the children of Israel (Bekh VIII 1 R Jose the Galilean)

18. Ex XIII 7 ולא יראה לך and there shall not be seen of thine (Pes II 2)
19. Ex XIII 12 הזכרים לה' the males unto the Lord (Bekh II 6 R Jose the Galilean)
20. Ex XIII 12 הזכרים לה' whatever is male unto the Lord (Bekh II 6 opponents of R Jose the Galilean)
21. Ex XIII 13 פטר חמור the firstborn (born) of an ass (Bekh I 2)
22. Ex XV 1 ויאמרו לאמר and they said saying (as follows) (Soṭ V 4 R Aḳiba)
23. Ex XV 1 ויאמרו לאמר and they said (responding) to the prompting (Soṭ V 4 R Nehemiah)
24. Ex XXI 21 יום או יומים a (full)[a] day or rather[b] two periods[a] of day(-light) Zab II 3)
25. Ex XXI 22 ולא יהיה אסון ענוש יענש and (if) there be no fatality, then shall he be fined (Ket III 2)
26. Ex XXI 28 וכי יגח שור and if an ox will (of his own accord) gore (B Ḳam IV 4)
27. Ex XXI 35 את שור רעהו the ox of his fellow (B Ḳam IV 3)
28. Ex XXI 35 וגם את המת יחצון and also the (value of the) carcass shall they halve (B Ḳam III 9 R Meir)
29. Ex XXI 35 וגם את המת יחצון and also (the value of) the dead (ox) shall they halve B Ḳam III 9 R Judah)
30. Ex XXI 36 ולא ישמרנו and he will not watch him (B Ḳam IV 9 R Meir)
31. Ex XXI 36 ולא ישמרנו and he will not take precautions with him (B Ḳam IV 9 R Judah)
32. Ex XXI 37 תחת השור . . . תחת השה for an ox . . . for a lamb (B Ḳam VII 1)
33. Ex XXII 5 השדה the soil (B Ḳam VI 4)
34. Ex XXII 5 שלם ישלם המבעיר את הבערה the maker of the brand shall surely make restitution (B Ḳam VI 4 R Elazar b Azariah, R Eliezer and R Aḳiba)
35. Ex XXII 5 שלם ישלם המבעיר את הבערה the incendiary shall surely make restitution for the brand (B Ḳam VI 4 R Simon)
36. Ex XXII 20 וגר לא תונה ולא תלחצנו and a proselyte[a] thou shalt not torment[b] (mentally) nor press him (economically) (B Meṣ IV 10)
37. Ex XXII 28 מלאתך ודמעך לא תאחר Thou shalt not change the order[a] (in the setting aside of the contributions from) thy (first) full[b] fruit and thy mixture[c] (of produce with its heave-offerings) (Ter III 6)
38. Ex XXIII 2 לא תהיה אחרי רבים לרעת . . . אחרי רבים להטת Thou shalt not follow the majority[a] to do evil[b] (in justice) . . . After[c] the majority (the scales of justice) must be turned.[d] (Snh I 6)
39. Ex XXIII 5 עזב תעזב thou shalt continually unload (B Meṣ II 10)
40. Ex XXIII 5 עזב תעזב עמו thou shalt surely unload together with him (B Meṣ II 10)
41. Ex XXIII 14 שלש רגלים three times (Ḥag I 1 Shammaiites)
42. Ex XXIII 14 שלש רגלים three pilgrimage festivals (Ḥag I 1 Hillelites)
43. Ex XXIII 16 וחג הקציר בכורי מעשיך and the harvest festival at the time of the first-fruits of thy work (Bik I 3)

44. Ex XXIII 19 בכורי אדמתך the first-fruits of *thy* soil (Bik I 2)
45. Ex XXIII 19 בית ה׳ אלהיך into the house of the Lord thy God (Bik I 9)
46. Ex XXV 30 לחם פנים bread of corners (Men XI 4 b Zoma)
47. Ex XXV 30 תמיד continually (without interruption) (Men XI 7 anon.)
48. Ex XXV 30 תמיד constantly (Men XI 7 R Jose)
49. Ex XXVI 33 והבדילה הפרכת לכם בין הקדש ובין קדש הקדשים and the curtain shall divide for you between the holy and the holy of holies (Yoma V 1 R Jose)
50. Ex XXVI 33 והבדילה הפרכת לכם בין הקדש ובין קדש הקדשים and a curtain (for each) shall divide for you between the holy and the holy of holies (Yoma V 1 anon.)
51. Ex XXIX 27 אשר הונף ואשר הורם which was swung (to and fro) and lifted up (Men V 6)
52. Ex XXXIV 20 ופטר חמור and a firstborn ass (Bekh I 2)
53. Ex XXXIV 20 בשה with the young (of Kleinvieh) (Bekh I 4)
54. Ex XXXIV 21 בחריש ובקציר תשבת i. e. from plowing as well as harvesting thou shalt rest (Shebi I 4 R Ishmael)
55. Ex XXXIV 21 בחריש ובקציר תשבת but during plowing time or harvest thou shalt rest (even during the six days of work) (Shebi I 4 anon.)
56. Lev I 3 לרצנו with his consent (Arakh V 6)
57. Lev II 11 כל המנחה the entire meal-offering (Men V 2)
58. Lev IV 13 עדת the (judicial) council (Hor I 4)
59. Lev IV 13 ונעלם דבר and something was forgotten (Hor I 3)
60. Lev IV 23 אשר חטא בה that[a] wherein he sinned intentionally (Ker IV 3 R Eliezer)
61. Lev IV 23 אשר חטא בה that (one thing)[a] wherein he sinned (Ker IV 3 R Joshua)
62. Lev IV 28 על חטאתו for his (own) sin (Ker VI 7)
63. Lev V 2 או בנבלת שרץ טמא ונעלם ממנו והוא טמא or (he touch) the carcass of an unclean swarming thing and it be hidden from him, so that he is unclean (Shebu II 5 R Eliezer)
64. Lev V 2 או בנבלת שרץ טמא ונעלם ממנו והוא טמא or (he touch) the carcass of an unclean swarming thing and it be hidden from him that he is unclean (Shebu II 5 R Aḳiba)
65. Lev V 4 להרע או להיטיב to do evil or to do good (in the future) (Shebu III 5 R Ishmael)
66. Lev V 19 אשם הוא אשם אשם לה׳ It is a (regular) guilt-offering. He owes a debt unto the Lord (Sheḳ VI 6)
67. Lev VI 2 הוא העלה it is that which goes up (Zeb IX 1)
68. Lev VI 2 על מוקדה על המזבח on its firewood (which is) on the altar (Zeb IX 1 R Johua)
69. Lev VI 2 על מוקדה על המזבח on its firewood, (namely) on the altar (Zeb IX 1, Rabban Gamaliel)
70. Lev VII 12 על זבח התודה on such thanks-offering (Men VII 4)
71. Lev VII 14 אחד מכל קרבן one (whole cake) for every sacrifice (Men VII 2)

72. Lev VII 16 וכל מנחת כהן and any meal offering of a *priest* (Sheḳ I 4 Rabban Joḥanan b Zakkai)
73. Lev VII 16 וכל מנחת כהן and *any meal offering* of a priest (Sheḳ I 4 Priests)
74. Lev VII 34 ואתן אתם לאהרן and I gave them (only) to Aaron (Ḥull X 1)
75. Lev IX 22 אל above (Soṭ VII 6 || Tam VII 2 R Judah)
76. Lev XI 33 יטמא shall defile (Soṭ V 2 R Aḳiba)
77. Lev XI 33 יטמא shall be unclean (Soṭ V 2 Rabban Joḥanan b Zakkai)
78. Lev XI 38 וכי יתן מים על זרע and if water be put on seed (Makhsh I 3 Hillelites)
79. Lev XIII 12 לכל מראה עיני הכהן to the full sight of the eyes of the priest Neg II 3)
80. Lev XIII 18 שחין inflammation (Neg IX 1)
81. Lev XIII 23 צרבת השחין a scar of the inflammation (Neg IX 2)
82. Lev XIII 24 מכות a burn (Neg IX 1)
83. Lev XIII 30 דק diminutive (Neg X 1 R Aḳiba)
84. Lev XIII 30 דק thin (Neg X 1 R Joḥanan b Nuri)
85. Lev XIII 42 בקרחת או בגבחת in the bald spot of the hair of the pate or the bald spot of the beard (Neg X 10)
86. Lev XIV 21 ועשרון סלת אחד בלול בשמן למנחה ולג שמן and one tenth of fine-meal mixed with meal-offering oil, and a log of oil (Men IX 3 anon)
87. Lev XIV 21 ועשרון סלת אחד בלול בשמן ולג שמן and one tenth of fine-meal mixed with oil to a meal-offering and (its) log of oil (Men IX 3 R Eliezer b Jacob)
88. Lev XIV 29 והנותר . . יתן . . לכפר and what remains . . . he shall put . . in order to atone (Neg XIV 10 R Aḳiba)
89. Lev XIV 29 והנותר . . יתן . . לכפר—and what remains . . . he shall put . .—to atone . . . (Neg XIV 10 R Joḥanan b Nuri)
90. Lev XIV 35 כנגע something like a plague (Neg XII 5)
91. Lev XIV 36 ופנו את הבית . . ולא יטמא כל אשר בבית and they shall clear the house . . . and whatever is in the house will not become unclean (Neg XII 5 R Judah)
92. Lev XIV 36 ופנו את הבית . . ולא יטמא כל אשר בבית and they shall clear the house . . . so that whatever is in the house may not become unclean. (Neg XII 5 R Simon)
93. Lev XIV 42 ולקחו אבנים אחרות והביאו . . ועפר אחר יקח וטח את הבית and they (pl.) shall take other stones and bring (pl.) . . . and other dirt shall he (s.) take and plaster (s.) the house (Neg XII 6)
94. Lev XIV 53 אל פני השדה facing the field (Neg XIV 2)
95. Lev XVI 6 ביתו his household (Yoma I 1 R Judah)
96. Lev XVI 30 מכל חטאתיכם לפני ה' תטהרו Ye shall be cleansed of all your sins against the Lord (Yoma VIII 9)
97. Lev XIX 9 ולקט קצירך and the fallings of thy harvest (Peah IV 10)
98. Lev XIX 10 לא תעולל thou shalt not pluck the grapes that have no arm and do not hang down (Peah VII 4)
99. Lev XIX 10 ופרט כרמך and the fallings of thy vineyard (Peah VII 3)

100. Lev XIX 13 פעלת שכיר the compensation[a] for service of one that hires[b] (something) out (B Meṣ IX 12)
101. Lev XIX 16 לא תלך רכיל בעמיך thou shalt not go tale-bearing about thy colleagues[a] (Snh III 7)
102. Lev XIX 20 והפדה לא נפדתה and she was not completely redeemed (Ker II 5 R Aḳiba)
103. Lev XIX 20 והפדה לא נפדתה and she was not at all redeemed (Ker II 5 R Ishmael)
104. Lev XIX 28 וכתבת קעקע לא תתנו בכם אני ה' and tattoo-writing you shall not put on you. I am the Lord (Makh III 6 anon.)
105. Lev XIX 28 וכתבת קעקע לא תתנו בכם אני ה' and you shall not put on you any tattoo writing (of) "I am the Lord" (Makh III 6 R Simon)
106. Lev XXI 7 זונה prostituting (Yab VI 5 R Judah)
107. Lev XXI 7 זונה prostitute (Yab VI 5 opponents of R Judah)
108. Lev XXI 7 מאישה from her (legitimate) husband (Yab X 3)
109. Lev XXI 12 ומן המקדש לא יצא and from the holy city he shall not go out (Snh II 1 R Meir)
110. Lev XXI 12 ומן המקדש לא יצא and from the sanctuary he shall not go out (Snh II R Judah)
111. Lev XXI 18 חרם flatnosed (Bekh VII 3)
112. Lev XXI 20 מרוח אשך abnormal in his privy parts (Bekh VII 5 anon.)
113. Lev XXI 20 מרוח אשך of crushed testicles (Bekh VII 5 R Ishmael)
114. Lev XXI 20 מרוח אשך with air in his testicles (Bekh VII 5 R Aḳiba)
115. Lev XXI 20 מרוח אשך dark-colored (Bekh VII 5 R Ḥanina b Antigonos)
116. Lev XXI 20 גבן defective in his eyebrows (Bekh VII 2 anon.)
117. Lev XXI 20 גבן one that has a single eyebrow (Bekh VII 2 R Dosa)
118. Lev XXI 20 גבן hunch-backed (Bekh VII 2 R Ḥanina b Antigonos)
119. Lev XXII 14 ונתן לכהן את הקדש then he shall give unto the priest what is holy (Ter VI 6 R Eliezer)
120. Lev XXII 14 ונתן לכהן את הקדש then he shall give unto the priest the holy thing (referred to) (Ter VI 6 R Aḳiba)
121. Lev XXII 28 ביום אחד on one (and the same full legal) day (of 24 hours) (Ḥull V 5)
122. Lev XXIII 4 אשר תקראו אתם במועדם *those which you shall proclaim in their season* (R Hash I 9)
123. Lev XXIII 4 אשר תקראו אתם *those* (only) that you shall proclaim (R Hash II 9 R Aḳiba)
124. Lev XXIII 14 עד up to (but not including) (Men X 5 Rabban Joḥanan b Zakkai)
125. Lev XXIII 14 עד up to (and including) (Men X 5 R Judah)
126. Lev XXIII 44 וידבר and he discussed (Meg III 6)
127. Lev XXIV 2 כתית למאור crushed for lighting (Men VIII 5)
128. Lev XXIV 5 ואפית and thou shalt sift (Men VI 7 R Simon)
129. Lev XXIV 7 על on (Men XI 5 opponents of Abba Saul)
130. Lev XXIV 7 על beside (i. e. over against) (Men XI 5 Abba Saul)

131. Lev XXIV 22 . . . משפט אחד יהיה לכם a[a] uniform court procedure[b] shall you have (Snh IV 1)
132. Lev XXV 15 שני תבואות (plural) years of crops (Arakh IX 1)
133. Lev XXV 27 לאיש אשר מכר לו to him to whom he sold it (Arakh IX 2a)
134. Lev XXV 27 לאיש אשר מכר לו to the (present) owner to whom one sold it (Arakh IX 2b)
135. Lev XXV 30 שנה תמימה a full (leap) year (Arakh IX 3 anon.)
136. Lev XXV 30 שנה תמימה a complete (solar) year (Arakh IX 3 Rabbi)
137. Lev XXV 30 לצמיתת in perpetuity (Arakh IX 4)
138. Lev XXV 33 כי בתי ערי הלוים for the houses of the cities of the Levites (Arakh IX 8 Rabbi)
139. Lev XXV 33 כי בתי ערי הלוים for the houses of the Levitical cities (Arakh IX 8 opponents of Rabbi)
140. Lev XXV 34 הוא is *it* (Arakh VIII 5 Rabbi)
141. Lev XXV 36 נשך ותרבית usury and increase (B Meṣ V 1)
142. Lev XXVII 7 מבן ששים שנה ומעלה over sixty years of age (Arakh IV 4)
143. Lev XXVII 10 טוב ברע או רע בטוב faultless for defective or defective for faultless (Tem I 2)
144. Lev XXVII 10 לא יחליפנו ולא ימיר אתו *he* should not exchange nor substitute it (Tem I 6)
145. Lev XXVII 10 הוא ותמורתו יהיה קדש it as well as its substitute should be holy (Tem I 1 R Aḳiba)
146. Lev XXVII 10 והיה הוא ותמורתו then it and whatever be substituted for it (Tem I 2 anon.)
147. Lev XXVII 10 והיה הוא ותמורתו then it and the (sacrificial beast) substituted for it (Tem I 2 R Simon b Elazar)
148. Lev XXVII 21 כשדה החרם לכהן תהיה אחזתו the possession thereof shall be the priest's like the field devoted (Arakh VIII 6 opponents of R Judah b Bathyra)
149. Lev XXVII 22 אשר לא משדה אחזתו which is not (part) of his hereditary land (Arakh VII 5 R Meir)
150. Lev XXVII 22 אשר לא משדה אחזתו which is not of the character of his hereditary land (Arakh VII 5 R Judah and R Simon)
151. Lev XXVII 28 כל חרם קדש קדשים הוא לה' Every devoted thing is most holy unto the Lord (Arakh VIII 6 R Judah b Bathyra)
152. Lev XXVII 28 כל חרם קדש קדשים הוא לה' Every devoted thing consisting of holy of holies belongs unto the Lord (Arakh VIII 6 opponents of R Judah b Bathyra)
153. Lev XXVII 32 וצאן and Kleinvieh (Bekh IX 1)
154. Num II 20 ועליו and beside him (Men XI 5 Abba Saul)
155. Num V 8 האשם המושב לה' לכהן the indebtedness[a] that is returned unto the Lord (reverts) to the priest[b] (B Ḳam IX 11)
156. Num V 13 ועד אין בה and there is no (complete) testimony against her Soṭ VI 3)
157. Num V 22 אמן אמן Amen, amen . . . . (Soṭ II 5 anon.)

158. Num V 22 אמן אמן Amen, (and) amen! (Soṭ II 5 R Meir)
159. Num V 23 בספר on a scroll (Soṭ II 4)
160. Num V 26 ואחר and hereafter (Soṭ III 2 R Simon)
161. Num V 26 ואחר and afterwards (Soṭ III 2)
162. Num V 29 ונטמאה and she (also) became unclean (Soṭ V 1 R Aḳiba)
163. Num V 29 ונטמאה so that she becomes unclean (Soṭ V 1 R Joshua)
164. Num VI 12 והימים הראשנים יפלו and *first* days will fall (Naz III 5 anon.)
165. Num VI 12 והימים הראשנים יפלו and the first *days* will fall (Naz III 5 R Eliezer)
166. Num VIII 8 שני two-year old (Parah I 2 R Jose the Galilean)
176. Num VIII 8 שני second (Parah I 2 opponents of R Jose the Galilean)
168. Num IX 10 דרך רחקה a distant way (Pes IX 2 R Aḳiba)
169. Num IX 10 דרך רחקה a way removed (from the Temple) (Pes IX 2 R Eliezer and R Jose)
170. Num XI 16 שבעים . . . עמך seventy . . . beside thee (Snh I 6 anon.)
171. Num XI 16 שבעים . . . עמך seventy . . . together with thee (Snh I 6 R Judah)
172. Num XIV 27 לעדה הרעה הזאת אשר המה מלינים עלי for this wicked congregation that causes murmuring[a] against Me. (Snh I 6)
173. Num XIV 35 במדבר הזה יתמו ושם ימתו in this wilderness will they perish and yonder will they die (Snh X 3 R Aḳiba)
174. Num XIV 35 במדבר הזה יתמו ושם ימתו in this wilderness will they perish and there (too) will they die (Snh X 3 R Eliezer)
175. Num XV 29 לעשה בשגגה for him who acts unwittingly (Ker I 2)
176. Num XVI 33 ויאבדו and they were exterminated (Snh X 3 R Aḳiba)
177. Num XVI 33 ויאבדו and they strayed (Snh X 3 R Eliezer)
178. Num XVIII 15 אך פדה תפדה but thou must assuredly redeem (Bekh VIII 8)
179. Num XXVIII 19, 20 תמימים יהיו לכם. ומנחתם faultless shall they be unto you as well as their meal offerings. (Men VIII 7)
180. Num XXVIII 31 תמימים יהיו לכם ונסכיהם faultless shall *they* be for you as well as their libations. (Men VIII 7)
181. Num XXX 10 ונדר אלמנה וגרושה and the vow (assumed) by (one who is) a widow or a divorcee (Ned XI 9)
182. Num XXX 14 אישה יקימנו ואישה יפירנו her husband may let it stand as well as he may nullify it (Ned X 7 opponents of R Eliezer)
183. Num XXX 14 אישה יקימנו ואישה יפירנו her husband may let stand or her husband may nullify it (Ned X 7 R Eliezer)
184. Num XXXV 13 שש ערי מקלט תהיינה six cities of refuge shall come into being (Makh II 4)
185. Num XXXV 24.25 . . . ושפטו העדה . . . והצילו העדה and the congregation[a] (of at least 10) shall condemn[b] . . . and the congregation shall save from sentence (Snh I 6)

186. Dt IV 9 ושמר נפשך מאד פן תשכח את הדברים אשר ראו עיניך and guard thy life very much lest thou forget the words[a] which thine eyes have seen (Ab III 8)
187. Dt VI 5 ובכל מאדך and with all thy wealth (Ber IX 5)
188. Dt VI 5 ובכל מאדך and with whatever thy measure (Ber IX 5 other interpretation a)
189. Dt VI 5 ובכל מאדך and with all thy gratitude (Ber IX 5 other interpretation b)
190. Dt VI 5 ובכל מאדך and with all thy might (Ber IX 5 other interpretation c)
191. Dt VI 7 בדרך in (thy) manner (Ber I 3 Hillelites)
192. Dt VI 7 ובשכבך ובקומך and whilest thou liest down and whilest thou risest up (Ber I 3 Shammaiites)
193. Dt VI 7 ובשכבך ובקומך and when thou liest down and when thou risest up (Ber I 3 Hillelites)
194. Dt VII 25 כסף וזהב עליהם gold and silver (which is) on them (Ab Zar III 5 anon.)
195. Dt VII 26 תועבה "abomination" (Ab Zar I 9)
196. Dt VII 26 שקץ תשקצנו thou shall surely regard it as a reptile (Ab Zar III 6 anon.)
197. Dt XI 30 אלוני מרה Elone More (Soṭ VII 5)
198. Dt XII 2 אלהיהם על ההרים הרמים ועל הגבעות their gods (which are) on the lofty mountains and the hills (Ab Zar III 5 R Jose the Galilean)
199. Dt XII 27 עלתיך הבשר והדם thy burnt-offerings (i. e.) the flesh and the blood. (Zeb IX 5)
200. Dt XIII בני בליעל people that will not be resurrected (Snh X 4)
201. Dt XIII 17 תוך רחובה her middle of the street (Snh X 6)
202. Dt XIII 17 רחובה its (own) broad place (Snh X 6)
203. Dt XIII 17 שללה *its* spoil (Snh X 6)
204. Dt XIII 17 כליל לה' אלהיך (like) a whole burnt-offering unto the Lord thy God (Snh X 6)
205. Dt XIII 17 לא תבנה עוד it shall never again be built (Snh X 6 R Jose)
206. Dt XIII 17 לא תבנה עוד it shall not be rebuilt (Snh X 6 R Aḳiba)
207. Dt XIII 18 לא . . . מאומה not . . . the least particle (Ab Zar III 3 opponents of R Jose)
208. Dt XIII 18 לא . . . מאומה not . . . a particle of consequence (Ab Zar III 3 R Jose)
209. Dt XIV 21 גדי young (of domesticated cattle) (Ḥull VIII 4 R Aḳiba)
210. Dt XIV 21 גדי young (mammal) (Ḥull VIII 4 R Jose the Galilean)
211. Dt XV 2 דבר השמטה the word of "release" (Shebi X 8)
212. Dt XVI 2 וזבחת פסח לה' אלהיך צאן ובקר and thou shalt slaughter a Passover sacrifice unto the Lord thy God, (as well as) sheep and cattle (Men VII 6)
213. Dt XVI 3 כל ימי חייך the *entire days* of thy life (Ber I 5 b Zoma)

214. Dt XVI 3 כל ימי חייך the entire duration of thy life (Ber I 5 opponents of b Zoma)
215. Dt XVI 17 איש כמתנת ידו כברכת ה' אלהיך אשר נתן לך every man like the gift of his hand like the blessing of the Lord thy God which he has given thee (Ḥag I 5)
216. Dt XVII 6 על פי שנים עדים upon the warning of two witnesses (Makk I 9 R Jose)
217. Dt XVII 6 על פי שנים עדים upon the direct oral testimony of two witnesses (Makk I 9 other interpretation)
218. Dt XVII 12 והאיש אשר יעשה בזדון and the man who out of presumption shall authorize action (Snh XI 2)
219. Dt XVII 13 וכל העם ישמעו and the entire people shall hear (it) (Snh XI 4 R Aḳiba)
220. Dt XVII 13 וכל העם ישמעו and the entire people shall hear of (it) (Snh XI 4 R Judah)
221. Dt XVII 15 שום תשים עליך מלך then shalt surely set a king above thee (Snh II 5)
222. Dt XVII 16 לו for his personal use (Snh II 4)
223. Dt XVII 17 ולא ירבה לו נשים and he shall not take unto him an excessive number of wives (Snh II 4 anon.)
224. Dt XVII 17 ולא ירבה לו נשים. ולא יסור ולבב and he shall not take unto himself many wives in order that his heart may not turn aside. (Snh II 4 Judah)
225. Dt XVII 17 ולא ירבה לו נשים ולא יסור לבבו and he shall not take unto himself a plural number of wives and his heart should not turn aside (Snh II 4 R Simon)
226. Dt XVII 17 לו for his (personal) use (Snh II 4)
227. Dt XVIII 11 אוב וידעוני a ventriloquist and one that produces speech with a magic bone in the mouth (Snh VII 7)
228. Dt XIX 3 תכין לך הדרך thou shalt make a direct road for thyself (Makk II 5)
229. Dt XIX 4 וזה דבר הרוצח and this is the word (spoken) by the murderer (Makk II 5)
230. Dt XIX 4 דבר הרוצח the word of "the murderer" (Shebi X 8 || Makk II 8)
231. Dt XIX 5 ואשר and as when . . . . (Makk II 2 anon. and Abba Saul)
232. Dt XIX 21 נפש בנפש life for life (taken) (Makk I 6 Sadducees)
233 Dt XIX 21 נפש בנפש life for life (condemned) (Makk I 6 Sages)
234. Dt XX 2 הכהן "*the* Priest" (Soṭ VIII 1)
235. Dt XX 2.3 ודבר אל העם. ואמר אלהם and he shall speak unto the people, saying to them (the following): (Soṭ VIII 1)
236. Dt XX 4 כי ה' אלהיכם ההלך עמכם for the Lord your God is he that accompanieth you (in a figurative sense) etc. (Soṭ VIII 1a)
237. Dt XX 4 כי ה' אלהיכם ההלך עמכם for (it is) the (symbol of the) Lord your God that walketh with you etc. (Soṭ VIII 1b)

238. Dt XX 5 כרם an orchard (Soṭ VIII 2)
239. Dt XX 8 ירא timid (Soṭ VIII 5 R Aḳiba)
240. Dt XX 8 ירא conscience-stricken (Soṭ VIII 5 R Jose the Galilean and R Jose)
241. Dt XXI 1 באדמה . . . נפל בשדה on the surface . . . lying on the soil (Soṭ IX 2)
242. Dt XXI 2 זקניך ושפטיך thy elders,[a] namely[b] thy judges[c] (Soṭ IX 1 anon.)
243. Dt XXI 2 זקניך ושפטך thy elders[a] and[b] (also) thy judges[c] (Soṭ IX 1 R Judah)
244. Dt XXI 4 איתן rugged (Soṭ IX 5)
245. Dt XXI 8 כפר . . . ישראל ונכפר להם הדם "Forgive . . . . Israel" And the blood shall be atoned unto them. (Soṭ IX 6)
246. Dt XXI 18 בן a male child (Snh VIII 1)
247. Dt XXI 20 בננו זה our son here (Snh VIII 4a)
248. Dt XXI 20 בננו זה this (same) son of ours (Snh VIII 4b)
249. Dt XXI 20 זולל וסבא (wine) drunkard and (meat) glutton (Snh VIII 2)
250. Dt XXI 23 קללת אלהים תלוי the cursing of God is (punished by being) hanged (Snh VI 4a)
251. Dt XXI 23 קללת אלהים תלוי a hanged man is a slighting of God (Snh VI 4b)
252. Dt XXI 23 קללת אלהים תלוי a hanged man occasions pain to God (Snh VI 5 R Meir)
253. Dt XXII 1 השב תשיבם thou shalt continually restore them (B Meṣ II 9)
254. Dt XXII 2 עד דרש אחיך אתו until the examination (by thee) of thy brother concerning it (B Meṣ II 7)
255. Dt XXII 2 והשבותו לו in order that they mayest[a] return it to him[b] (B Meṣ II 7)
256. Dt XXII 6 קן צפור . . . אפרחים או ביצים a bird-nest . . . chick or egg (Ḥull XII 2)
257. Dt XXII 7 שלח תשלח את האם thou shalt continually release the mother Ḥull XII 2)
258. Dt XXII 7 שלח תשלח את האם thou shalt surely send away the mother (Ḥull XII 3)
259. Dt XXII 11 שעטנז what is fulled and spun and woven (Kil IX 8 anon.)
260. Dt XXII 11 שעטנז what is fulled and spun and twisted (Kil IX 8 R Simon b Elazar)
261. Dt XXII 29 ולו תהיה לאשה if[a] she be a wife (suitable) for him (Ket III 5)
262. Dt XXIII 2 פצוע דכה וכרות שפכה one who is wounded in his testicles and whose penis is torn (Yab VII 2)
263. Dt XXIII 2 לא יבא . . . בקהל ה' he shall not enter into nuptial relationship with the congregation of the Lord (Yab VIII 2)
264. Dt XXIII 19 אתנן זונה ומחיר כלב a harlot's hire and the exchange of a dog (Tem VI 2)
265. Dt XXIII 19 בית ה' אלהיך up to the house of the Lord thy God (Parah II 3 anon.)

266. Dt XXIII 19 בית ה' אלהיך into the house of the Lord thy God (Parah II 3 R Eliezer)
267. Dt XXIII 19 גם שניהם *even* the *two* of *them* (Tem VI 3)
268. Dt XXIV 1 ערות דבר substantiated[a] unchastity (Soṭ VI 3)
269. Dt XXIV 1 כי מצא בה ערות דבר because he found in her an instance of unchastity (Giṭṭ IX 10 Shammaiites)
270. Dt XXIV 1 כי מצא בה ערות דבר because he found in her unchastity, aye anything (Giṭṭ IX 10 Hillelites)
271. Dt XXIV 1 כי מצא בה ערות דבר as when he found in her an instance of unchastity (Giṭṭ IX 10 R Aḳiba)
272. Dt XXIV 1 וכתב לה then he shall write for her (Giṭṭ III 2)
273. Dt XXIV 6 נפש sustenance (B Meṣ IX 13)
274. Dt XXIV 7 והתעמר בו and he employ him as a slave (Snh XI)
275. Dt XXIV 15 שכרו his hire (B Meṣ IX 12)
276. Dt XXIV 17 בגד אלמנה the dress of (belonging to) a widow (B Meṣ 13)
277. Dt XXIV 21 כי תבצר כרמך לא תעולל if thou[a] gatherest the grapes of thy vineyard, thou shalt not glean[b] (Peah VII 7 R Eliezer)
278. Dt XXIV 21 כי תבצר כרמך לא תעולל When[a] thou gatherest the grapes of thy vineyard thou shalt not pluck gleanings[b] (Peah VII 7 R Aḳiba)
279. Dt XXV 2 והפילו and he shall incline him (Makk VIII 13)
280. Dt XXV 2.3 והכהו . . . כדי רשעתו במספר. ארבעים יכנו and he shall smite him—according to his wickedness. Up to the number of forty (stripes) shall he smite him (Makk III 10 anon.)
281. DtXXV 2.3 והכהו . . . כדי רשעתו במספר. ארבעים יכנו and he shall smite him—according to his wickedness by number. Forty (stripes) shall he smite him (Makk III 10 R Judah)
282. Dt XXV 3 ונקלה אחיך לעיניך Once[a] he is flogged,[b] he shall be a brother (again) in thine eyes (Makk III 15)
283. Dt XXV 5 . . . ומת אחד מהם if a single one of them die . . . then etc. (Yab III 9)
284. Dt XXV 7.8 ועלתה יבמתו . . . ואמרה . . . לא אבה יבמי. וקראו לו זקני עירו ודברו אליו . . . ואמר לא חפצתי לקחתה

And his sister-in-law will go up . . . and say: ". . . he does not wish to take me as a levirate-wife"— and the elders of his city had called him and spoken to him— and he . . will say: "I do not desire to take her" (Yab XII 6)
285. Dt XXV 9 בפניו before him (Yab XII 6)
286. Dt XXV 9 וענתה ואמרה and she shall repeat and say (the following) (Soṭ VII 3 anon.)
287. Dt XXV 9 ואמרה ככה and she shall say: "Thus . . . (Soṭ VII 4 anon.)
288. Dt XXV 9 ואמרה ככה and she shall say thus: ". . . . (Soṭ VII 4 R Judah)
289. Dt XXV 10 . . . ונקרא שמו בישראל בית and his name shall be proclaimed unto Israel as the house etc. (Yab XII 6 anon.)
290. Dt XXV 10 ונקרא שמו בישראל בית and his name shall be proclaimed by Israel as the house etc. (Yab XII 6 R Judah)

291. Dt XXVI 5 וענית ואמרת לפני ה' אלהיך and thou shalt repeat and say before the Lord thy God (the following)) Soṭ VII 3)
292. Dt XXVI 14 באני when I was in mourning (Maas Sh V 12)
293. Dt XXVI 14 בטמא when unclean (Maas Sh V 12)
294. Dt XXVI 14 למת for the dead (Maas Sh V 12)
295. Dt XXVII 8 באר היטב perfectly translated (Soṭ VII 5)
296. Dt XXVII 14 וענו הלוים ואמרו and the Levites shall repeat and say (the following): (Soṭ VII 3 4)
297. Dt XXIX 27 כיום הזה like[a] this[b] here day (Snh X 3 R Eliezer)
298. Dt XXIX 27 כיום הזה like[a] this[b] (present) day (Snh X 3 R Aḳiba)
299. Dt XXXI 10 מקץ שבע שנים במעד שנת השמטה בחג הסכת after[a] the end[b] of seven years on the holiday[c] (following) the year of release on the feast of booths (Soṭ VII 8)
300. Dt XXXIII 21 כי שם חלקת מחקק ספון . . . צדקת ה' עשה for there the portion of the Lawgiver[a] is buried . . the righteousness of the Lord he performed . . . . (Ab V 18)
301. Jos VI 5 שופר ramshorn (R Hash III 2 anon.)
302. Jos VI 5 שופר horn (R Hash III 2 R Jose)
303. Jos VII 25 ביום הזה on *this* day (Snh VI 2)
304. Jos VIII 33 נגד הכהנים הלוים opposite the priests (were) the Levites . . . (Soṭ VII 5)
305. Jud XIII 5 ומורה and a razor (Naz IX 5 R Nehorai)
306. I Sam I 11 ומורה and a razor etc. (Naz IX 5 R Nehorai)
307. I Sam I 11 ומורה and fear etc. (Naz IX 5 R Jose)
308. I Sam XXV 18 צאן (pl.) sheep (Ḥull XI 2 Hillelites)
309. I Sam XVII 36 הערל the "Uncircumcised" (Ned III 11)
310. II Sam I 20 הערלים the "Uncircumcised" (Ned III 11)
311. Is VII 21 צאן (pl.) sheep (Ḥull XI 2 Shammaiites)
312. Is XXV 8 בלע המות לנצח He will destroy death forever (M Ḳaṭ III 9)
313. Is XXVIII 8 בלי מקום without (the) Infinite (Ab III 3)
314. Is XXIX 1 הוי אריאל אריאל קרית חנה דוד Oh lion-(shaped house of) God[a], lion-(shaped house of) God, in the[b] city in which David camped (Midd IV 7)
315. Is XXX 22 תזרם כמו דוה separate[a] them like a menstruant[b] (Sabb IX 1 || Ab Zar III 6 R Aḳiba)
316. Is XLI 4 קרא הדרות מראש that calleth the generations earlier (Ed II 9)
317. Is XLII 21 יגדיל He will make large (Makk III 16 R Ḥananyah b Aḳashyah)
318. Is XLV 18 לשבת for populating (Giṭṭ IV 5 || Ed I 13 Shammaiites)
319. Is LVIII 8 והלך לפניך צדקך כבוד ה' יאספך if[a] thy righteousness will precede thee, the glory of the Lord will bury[b] thee (Soṭ I 9)
320. Is LX 21 לעולם יירשו ארץ in the world everlasting they will inherit (the) earth (Snh X 1)
321. Is LXVI 23 מדי חדש בחדשו the interval between a month and its recurrence (Ed II 10 anon)

322. Is LXVI 23 מדי שבת בשבתו the interval between a festival (and another falling) at (the conclusion of) its (seven) week (cycle) (Ed II 10 R Joḥanan b Nuri)
323. Jer IX 19 קינה antiphonic lament (M Ḳaṭ III 9)
324. Jer IX 25 ערלים "Uncircumcised" (Ned III 11)
325. Jer XIV 8 מקוה purification bath (Yoma VIII 9 R Aḳiba)
326. Jer XVII 7 ברוך הגבר אשר יבטח בה׳ והיה ה׳ מבטחו Blessed[a] (with wealth) will be the man who relies (for his sustenance) on the Lord so that the Lord will become his hope[b] (Peah VII 9)
327. Jer XXXIII 25 אם לא בריתי יומם ולילה were it not for My covenant[a] (of circumcision) (which operates) by day and by night[b] (Ned III 11)
328. Ez XLI 23 ושתים דלתות להיכל ולקדש and two doors (apiece) for the hall and the holy (Midd IV 1)
329. Ez XLIII 16 שתים עשרה ארך בשתים עשרה רחב רבוע אל ארבעת רבעיו twelve in length and twelve in width, square, (thus) in (each of) its four quarters (Midd III 1)
330. Ez XLVI 22 קטרות roofless (Midd II 5)
331. Hosea IV 14 לא אפקד I shall not *examine*[a] (Soṭ IX 9 R Joḥanan)
332. Joel II 23 בראשון on[a] the first[b] (month) (Taan I 2 R Meir)
333. Amos IX 6 ואגדתו and his bundle (Ab III 6)
334. Ps I 5 על כן לא יקמו רשעים במשפט וחטאים בעדת צדיקים Therefore (the) "wicked"[a] shall not stand for *the* (final) judgment,[b] nor "sinners"[c] in the congregation of (the) righteous (Snh X 3 R Nehemiah)
335. Ps I 5 על כן לא יקמו רשעים במשפט וחטאים בעדת צדיקים Therefore (the) "wicked"[a] shall have no existence in the judgment[b] (of the righteous), nor "sinners"[c] in the congregation of (the) righteous (Snh X 3 opponents of R Nehemiah)
336. Ps XXV 14 סוד secret (Yad IV 3 R Eliezer)
337. Ps XL 3 היון the cistern (Miḳw IX 2)
338. Ps LXVIII 27 במקהלות in congregations (Ber VII 3 R Jose the Galilean)
339. Ps LXVIII 27 במקהלות in chorus (Ber VII 3 R Aḳiba)
340. Ps LXXXII 1 בעדת אל with a godly congregation (of at least ten) (Ab III 6)
341. Ps LXXXII 1 אלהים judges (Ab III 6)
342. Ps CXIX 99 מכל מלמדי השכלתי I have obtained understanding from[a] all them that taught me (Ab IV 1)
343. Ps CXIX 126 עת לעשות לה׳ הפרו תורתך It is time to do for the Lord because they have broken Thy Law (Ber IX 5 anon.)
344. Ps CXIX 126 עת לעשות לה׳ הפרו תורתך When it is time to do for the Lord, they have broken Thy Law (Ber IX 5 R Nathan)
345. Ps CXXVII 2 יגיע כפיך כי תאכל אשריך וטוב לך If[a] thou wilt eat the toil of thine hands thou wilt be rich[b] and it will be well with thee (Ab IV 1)
346. Pr IV 2 תורתי my Torah (Ab III 14)
347. Pr XI 27 רעה misfortune (Peah VIII 9)

348. Job I 1) וירא אלהים and afraid of God (Soṭ V 5 Rabban Joḥanan b Zakkai)
349. Job XIII 15 הן יקטלני לא איחל behold if he slay me I hope for him (Soṭ V 5 R Joshua b Hyrkanos)
350. Job XIII 15 הן יקטלני לא איחל behold if he slay me I do not hope (Soṭ V 5 R Joḥanan b Zakkai[a])
351. Cant I 2 דדיך thy(m.) love (Ab Zar II 5 R Joshua)
352. Cant I 2 דדיך thy teats (Ab Zar II 5 R Ishmael)
353. Lam III 28 ישב בדד וידם כי נטל עליו He that sitteth alone and silently meditates, verily he receiveth (reward) for it (Ab III 2)
354. Eccl I 15 מעות לא יוכל לתקן what is crooked cannot be made straight (Ḥag I 7 R Simon b Menasyah)
355. Eccl I 15 מעות לא יוכל לתקן what has been twisted cannot be made straight (Ḥag I 7 R Simon b Jochai)
356. II Chr XXXIII 13 ויתפלל אליו ויעתר לו . . . וישיבהו ירושלם למלכותו and he prayed to Him and He was entreated by him . . . and He (also) restored him to Jerusalem to his kingdom (Snh X 2 R Judah)
357. II Chr XXXIII 13 ויתפלל אליו ויעתר לו . . . וישיבהו ירושלם למלכותו and he prayed to Him and He was entreated by him . . so that He restored him to Jerusalem to his kingdom (Snh X 2 opponents of R Judah)

NOTES I

[1] "dass den Weisen des Talmuds grammatisches Bewusstsein durchaus nicht gefehlt hat und bei ihnen, wenn sie auch über den streng wissenschaftlichen Apparat nicht verfügten, Beiträge für die Geschichte der Schrift, der Sprache, für das Nomen and Verbum, für die Partikeln, für Etymologien, für Sprachvergleichungen und Synonymen, ja sogar für grammatische Termen zu gewinnen seien."

[2] Die einfache Bibelexegese der Tannaim, *L. Dobschütz*, Breslau, 1893.

[3] Cf. *Bacher* in the Jewish Encyclopedia, New York and London 1903, article Bible Exegesis.

[4] *Georg Aicher*, Das alte Testament in der Mischna, Freiburg im Breisgau 1906.

[5] מאיר ליבוש מלבי"ם, התורה והמצוה, ווילנא תרפ"ח A work of a similar nature is הכתב והקבלה, a commentary on the Pentateuch by Jacob Zebi Meklenburg, the 4th edition of which was published in Frankfort on the Main in 1880.

[6] Cf. *I. H. Weiss*, Zur Geschichte der jüdischen Tradition, Vilna 1904, II chapter 19 and III chapter 1 ff.

[7] The following clear instances of the reconciliation of alleged contradictions may be noted in the Mishnah.

Peah VII 7 Lev XIX 10 וכרמך לא תעולל vs Dt XXIV 21 . . . כי תבצר כרמך לא תעולל
Shek VI 6 Lev V 19a אשם הוא vs b אשם אשם לה'.
Soṭ V 3 Num XXXV 4 אלף אמה vs 5 אלפים באמה
Snh I 6 Ex XXIII 2a לא תהיה אחרי רבים לרעת vs c אחרי רבים להטת
Makk I 6 Dt XIX 19 ועשיתם לו כאשר זמם vs 21 נפש בנפש
Ed II 9 Gen XV 13 וענו אתם ארבע מאות שנה vs 16 ודור רביעי ישובו הנה
Zeb IX 5 Lev I 9 והקטיר הכהן את הכל המזבחה עלה vs Dt XII 27 ועשית עלתיך הבשר והדם

The contradiction in this instance is more fully expressed in Sa Lev I 9 which is also quoted in b Zeb 85b ff.

Men VII 6 Ex XII 5 מן הכבשים ומן העזים תקחו vs Dt XVI 2 וזבחת פסח לה' אלהיך צאן ובקר
Arakh VIII 6 Lev XXVII 22 כשדה החרם לכהן תהיה אחזתו vs 28 כל חרם קדש קדשים הוא לה'
Arakh VIII 7 Lev XXVII 26 אך בכור . . . לא יקדיש vs Dt XV 19 . . . כל הבכור תקדיש

The inconceivability of contradiction on the part of the Tannaim is clearly reflected by such expressions as: אי אפשר לומר . . . שכבר נאמר (Soṭ V 3, Arakh VIII 7), אם כן למה נאמר (Peah VII 7, Snh I 6, Makk I 6, Men VII 6, Arakh VIII 6), and אף על פי שנאמר (Ed II 9).

The eagerness to reconcile is obvious from the declaration in Shek VI 6 of נמצאו ב' כתובים קיימים. Cf. also Dobschütz p. 39 ff.

[8] The following express cases in which such analogies are made are recorded in the Mishnah:
Soṭ VI 3 דבר Dt XXIV 1 = דבר Dt XIX 15
Soṭ VII 3 ענה Dt XXIV 5 = ענה Dt XXVII 14
Soṭ VII 4 ענה Dt XXV 9 = ענה Dt XXVII 14
Soṭ VII 5 אלוני מרה Dt XI 30 = אלון מורה Gen XII 6
Snh I 6 עדה Num XXXV 24, 25 = עדה Num XIV 27
Men XI 5 על Lev XXIV 7 = על Num II 20
Ḥull V 5 יום אחד Lev XXII 28 = יום אחד Gen I 5

The application of Gen VI 3 to the generation of the flood (Snh X 3) also indicates that the Pentateuch was regarded as a unit.

[9] Cf. Snh VIII 2 זולל וסבא Dt XXI 20 = סבאי . . . זוללי. Pr XXIII 20
Ḥull XI 2 צאן Dt XVIII 4 = צאן Is VII 21 (Shammaiites) צאן I Sam XXV 18 (Hillelites).

The remark ואף על פי שאין ראיה לדבר זכר לדבר has reference to the authoritativeness of the extralegal portions of the Bible such as the Prophets and the Hagiographa as sources of law, not as indications of the usage of the word. Cf. the same remark in Sabb VIII 7 and IX 4 where it is not the question of the meaning of the words. The Babylonian Amoraim (Cf. b Sabb 134b) were uncertain about the meaning of זכר לדבר used in connection with Gen XXXIV 25. If our theory is correct this expression was used of this verse because it is contained in a narrative section of the Pentateuch. Cf. the list of passages with reference to which the formula זכר is used in Bacher's Exegetische Terminologie der jüdischen Traditionsliteratur, Leipzig 1905 I p. 51 ff. Not one passage is contained in the legal section of the Pentateuch.

[10] Cf. the remark of R. Nehorai in Ḳidd IV 14: מניח אני כל אומנות שבעולם ואיני מלמד בני אלא תורה שאדם אוכל משכרה בעולם הזה והקרן קיימת לעולם הבא and the biblical verses cited in support of it.

[11] Ps LXXXII 1.
[12] Amos IX 6.
[13] Mal III 16.
[14] Mal III 16 and Ex XX 24.
[15] Cf. Ab III 2 and 6.
[16] Lam III 28.
[17] Cf. Ab III 2.
[18] Ps XCII 13.
[19] Is XL 31.
[20] Cf. Kidd IV 14.
[21] ibid.

[22] Cf. Ber IX 5 with reference to Ruth II 4. Cf. also the remark in b Ber 63a: וכי תימא בעז מדעתיה דנפשיה קאמר.

[23] Sheḳ VI 6 זה מדרש דרש יהוידע כהן גדול.

[24] *Abraham* in Gen XX 7 and 17 (B Ḳam VIII 7)
Aaron in Lev IX 22 (Soṭ VII 6, Tam VII 2)
Reubenites and Gadites in Num XXXII 22 (Sheḳ III 3), in Num XXXII 29. 30 (Ḳidd III 4 Rabbi Meir)
Joshua in Jos VII 19.20 (Snh VI 2)
The Angel of Gideon in Jud VI 12 (Ber IX 5)
Boaz in Ruth II 4 (Ber IX 5)
David in II Sam III 31 (Snh II 3 R. Judah) in II Sam XII 8 (Snh II 2 R Judah) in I Chr XXIX 14 (Ab III 7)

Josiah in II Kings XXIII 9 (Men XXII 10)
Ezra in Ezra IV 3 (Sheḳ I 5)

[25] Cf. *Bacher*, Terminologie I p. 110 ff. article מועט for the sources and the meaning of this statement.

[26] Cf. ibid and
בראם Gen V 2 (Yab VI 6)
פרו ורבו Gen I 28 (Yab VI 6 R Joḥanan b Baroḳa)
ימים Num VI 12 (Naz III 5 R Eliezer)
זקניך ושפטיך Dt XXI 2 (Soṭ IX 1 R Judah)
הזכרים Ex XIII 12 (Bekh II 6 R Jose the Galilean)
שני Lev XXV 15 (Arakh IX 1)

[27] E. g. אדמתך Ex XXIII 19 = of thy soil, not what is not of thy soil (Bik I 2)
לך Ex XIII 7 = to Jews, but not to gentiles (Pes II 2). In MS this is stated more explicitly ולא יראה לך חמץ רואה אתה לאחרים.
ומת אחד מהם Dt XXV 5 = only where *one* died, not otherwise (Yab III 9)
מאישה Lev XXI 7 = only from one who is her legitimate husband, not from one who is not (Yab X 3)
ולא יהיה אסון ענוש יענש Ex XXI 22 = only he who has not caused death pays a money fine (Ket III 2)
באדמה . . . נפל בשדה Dt XXI 1 = the law applies only to the case where these conditions are fulfilled (Soṭ IX 2)
לה Dt XXIV 1 = expressly for her, not for anyone else (Giṭṭ III 2)
כי מצא בה ערות דבר Dt XXIV 1 = only such a one may be divorced (Giṭṭ IX 10)
רעהו Ex XXI 35 = only of his fellow, not that belonging to the sanctuary (B Ḳam IV 3)
כי יגח Ex XXI 28 = only one who gores by himself, not one who is incited (B Ḳam IV 4)
תחת השור . . . תחת השה Ex XXI 37 = the law applies only to oxen and sheep, not to other animals (B Ḳam VII 1). MS adds גזירת המלך
ושלחה ידה והחזיקה במבושיו. Dt XXV 11 = only in cases such as this is compensation paid for disgrace, not otherwise (B Ḳam VIII 1)
בן Dt XXI 18 = male child, not female or adult (Snh VIII 1) (Br in b Snh 69b and j [Cf. also MT] terms the use of the expression בן a גזירת הכתוב or גזירת המלך which is a very apt characterization of the principle of Tannaitic exegesis which this example illustrates)
זולל וסבא Dt XXI 20 = only to a glutton and a drunkard can the law of the wayward son be applied (Snh VIII 2)
שללה Dt XIII 17 = the property belonging to the city, not that of the sanctuary (Snh X 6)
כסף וזהב עליהם Dt VII 25 = the silver and gold in them, not they themselves (Ab Zar III 5)
אלהיהם על ההרים . . Dt XII 2 = their gods on the mountains, not the mountains themselves (Ab Zar III 5)

המקריב את הדם . . . ואת החלב Lev VII 33 = only one who fulfills these functions completely can receive the gifts, not one who does not (Zeb XII 1)

לכהן הזרק Lev VII 14 = only this goes to the priest, the rest belongs to the owner (Men VII 2)

על זבח התודה Lev VII 12 = only with the thanks-offering beast itself, not its child etc. (Men VII 4)

כתית למאור Lev XXIV 2 = it must be crushed only if used for lighting, not otherwise (Men VIII 5)

אתם Lev VII 34 = only them, nothing else (Ḥull X 1)

שלח תשלח את האם Dt XXII 7 = the law of releasing applies to the mother, not the children (Hull XII 3)

גם שניהם Dt XXIII 19 = only these two are forbidden, nothing else (Tem VI 3)

Note: It is to be observed that in most of the examples cited above the restriction is indicated by the use of an emphatic personal pronoun, a numeral, the infinitive absolute or some redundancy q. v. infra.

[28] E. g. בשכבך ובקומך Dt VI 7 = in a reclining and standing posture (Ber I 3 Shammaiites)

תביא בית ה' אלהיך Ex XXIII 19 = it must be brought into the Temple (Bik I 9)

אשר תקראו אתם במעדם Lev XXIII 4 = they must be proclaimed in their right season (R Hash I 9)

תשמרו להקריב Num XXVIII 2 = you are to watch over the offering of the sacrifices (Taan IV 2) (Se says explicitly: תשמרו, שיהו כהנים לוים וישראל עומדים עליהם)

וענית ואמרת Dt XXVI 5 i. e. the following words (Soṭ VII 3) (Cf. the remark of Rabbi Judah in Soṭ VII 4 וענתה ואמרה ככה עד שתאמר בלשון הזה which clearly indicates the underlying assumption, because he differs only in the derivation of the halakha not in the halakha itself)

וענו הלוים ואמרו Dt XXVII 14 i. e. the following words (Soṭ VII 4)

וענתה ואמרה Dt XXV 9 i. e. the following words (Soṭ VII 4)

ודבר Dt XX 2 i. e. the following words (Soṭ VIII 1)

ואת כל אשר בה Dt XIII 16 = all that is in it without exception (Snh X 5)

מאומה Dt XIII 18 = nothing, not even the least particle (Ab Zar III 3)

ואפית אתה Lev XXIV 5 = bake completely (Men VI 7)

תתן לו Dt XVIII 4 = give him something (Ḥull XI 2)

בית ה' אלהיך Dt XXIII 19 = they must not be brought within the temple building (Parah II 3 R Eliezer)

Extreme cases of this literalism are:

וכפר בעדו ובעד ביתו Lev XVI 6 = provision must be made that he has a wife to atone for (Yoma I 1 R Judah)

תקבץ אל תוך רחבה Dt XIII 17 = a broad place must be created to burn the spoil in (Snh X 6)

[29] E. g. בין הערבים Lev XXIII 5 = in the afternoon, not the forenoon (Pes V 3)

בספר Num V 23 = scroll, nothing else (Soṭ II 4)

נמחה Num V 23 = what can be erased, nothing else (Soṭ II 4)

איש אשר יתן לכהן לו והיה Num V 10 = it shall remain his, it may not be taken away again (B Ḳam IX 12)

בחוץ תעמד Dt XXIV 11 = he must remain outside, he may not come in. (B Meṣ IX 13)

ותפשו בו . . . Dt XXI 19.20 = the procedure must be carried out exactly in this way, not otherwise (Snh VIII 4). (Cf. the supposition of b Snh 71a שמעת מינה בעינן קרא כדכתיב which is refuted only by the remark that the redundancy of the verse indicates restriction שאני הכא דכוליה קרא יתירא הוא)

והפילו השופט Dt XXV 2 = he must lay him down. The flogging is not to be administered with the culprit being in some other posture (Makk III 13)

הוא העלה Lev VI 2 = it goes up and not down once up (Zeb IX 1)

אחד Lev VII 14 = one and not a fraction of one (Men VII 2)

וזבחת ואכלת Dt XXVII 7 = only what is slaughtered may be eaten, not anything killed by some other process (Ḥull II 3)

והביא קרבנו . . . על חטאתו Lev IV 28 = for his sin not for his father's sin (Ker VI 7)

ועפר אחר יקח וטח Lev XIV 42 = he alone engages in the plastering. No one may help him. (Neg XII 6)

[30] Cf. Bekh I 7

פדייה is preferred to עריפה because of Ex XIII 13 ואם לא תפדה וערפתו

יעידה is preferred to פדייה because of Ex XXI 8 אשר לא יעדה והפדה

גאולה is preferred to מכירה because of Lev XXVII 27 ואם לא יגאל ונמכר בערכך

[31] Cf. Ker VI 9 with regard to the status: of goats and lambs as indicated by Lev IV 32, of doves and turtle doves as indicated by Lev XII 6, of father and mother as indicated by Lev XIX.

[32] E. g. בעבור זה עשה ה' לי Ex XIII 8 = for every Jew individually (Pes X 5)

אבא אליך וברכתיך Ex XX 24 = thee, individually (Ab III 6)

תמורתו Lev XXVII 10 = its individual substitute (Tem I 2 R Simon b Elazar) Cf. Malbim hereon

לא יחליפנו ולא ימיר אתו Lev XXVII 10 = an individual may not exchange or substitute (Tem I 6)

ועפר אחר יקח וטח Lev XIV 42 = the leper alone, without any assistance (Neg XII 6)

(Malbim points out that the remark was caused by the change from the plural to the singular in the massoretic text. It is interesting to note that this difference does not exist in either S, V or Pš, although it is faithfully reflected by O and PJ)

[33] Cf. note 26 above and

מקהלות Ps LXVIII 27 (Ber VII 3 R Jose the Galilean). (The issue is made clear in j which asks מה מקיימין רבנן טעמא דר" יוסי הגלילי and answers: במקהלות בכל קהלה וקהלה i. e. according to them it is a generic, not, as R Jose would have it, a numerical plural)

תשמרו Num XXVIII 2 (Taan IV 2) i. e. all Jews individually are to superintend the sacrifices as is clearly stated in Se. Cf. note 28 above.

34 E. g. unnecessary personal pronouns or numerals q. v. infra and
כל in כל ימי חייך Dt XVI 3 (Ber I 5). (Cf. Malbim who points out that ימי חייך would have been sufficient to express the usual meaning).
כל in בכל לבבך ובכל נפשך ובכל מאדך Dt VI 5 (Ber IX 5)
לאמר after ויאמרו Ex XV 1 (Soṭ V 4)
(That the word is considered redundant and therefore requiring interpretation is evident from the remark שאין תלמוד לומר לאמר ומה תלמוד לומר לאמר Cf. also Rashi ad loc.)
ביום הזה Jos VII 25 (Snh VI 2)
במגפה לפני ה' after וימתו Num XIV 37 (Snh X 3)
With the exception of ביום הזה in Jos VII 25 (Snh VI 2) all of these redundancies are explained as extensions of the activity.

35 E. g. the infinitive absolute used with the finite verb q. v. infra and:
לאיש אשר for לאשר Lev XXV 27 (Arakh IX 2)
Sifra has the reading ת"ל ל א ש ר מכר לו . . . ת"ל לאיש
(Cf. the comment of Malbim who shows how the ambiguity redounds to the favor of the redeemer.)
מי האיש אשר for ומי אשר Dt XX 5.6.7 (Soṭ VIII 2)
(In Se the wider interpretation is explicitly based on the word האיש which the previous example has shown to be superfluous. Cf. also Malbim ad loc.)
כי נפש הוא חבל Dt XXIV 6 (B Meṣ IX 13) extends the preceding לא יחבל רחים ורכב showing that רחים and רכב were merely illustrations.

36 An extension in application is alleged to be indicated by the repetition of
ובאו Num V 22 and 24 (Soṭ V 1)
נטמאה Num V 13 and 27 (Soṭ V 1 Rabbi)
העדה Num XXV 24 and 25 (Snh I 6)
שמה Num XXXV 16, 25 and 26 (Makk II 7)
(In the Mishnah only Num XXXV 25 is cited but in Se Dt XIX 4 the threefold repetition is mentioned.)
ונעלם Lev V 2 and 3 (Shebu II 5 Rabbi Ishmael)
אשה ריח ניחח Lev I 9, 13 and 17 and Lev II 2 (Men XIII 11)
A restriction is alleged to be indicated by the emphasis inherent in the repetition of
אתם Lev XXIII 2, 4 and 37 (R Hash II 9)
(In the Mishnah only Lev XXIII 4 is cited but Br b R Hash 25a says explicitly: הרי הוא אומר אתם אתם אתם ג' פעמים אתם אפילו שוגגין אתם אפילו מזידין אתם אפילו מוטעין.
שור... שה twice in Ex XXI 37 (B Ḳam VII 1 Cf. comment of Malbim hereon)
התודה twice in Lev VII 12 (Men VII 4 Cf. comment of Malbim hereon)
גדי Ex XXIII 19, Ex XXXIV 26 and Dt XIV 21 (Ḥull VIII 4 R Aḳiba)
פטר חמור Ex XIII 13 and XXXIV 20 (Bekh I 2).

37 E. g. כל קהל || עדת || ישראל Ex XII 6 (Pes V 5)
אל ירך לבבכם || אל תיראו || אל תחפזו || אל תערצו Dt XX 3 (Soṭ VIII 1)
הירא || רך הלבב Dt XX 8 (Soṭ VIII 5)

רעים || חטאים Gen XIII 13 (Snh X 3)
אשריך || טוב לך Ps CXXVIII 2 (Ab IV 1)

[38] Examples of *repetition* all of which are interpreted as extensions of meaning are:

ויפץ ה' אתם משם על פני כל הארץ Gen XI 8 || ומשם הפיצם ה' על פני כל הארץ Gen XI 9 (Snh X 3)

את שלש הערים... ערי מקלט תהיינה Num XXXV 13 || שש ערי מקלט תהיינה לכם Num XXXV 14 (Makk II 4)

(Cf. Se Num XXXV 13 where the redundancy is noted and explained more fully)

Examples of *parallelism* are:

לא עברתי ממצותיך || ולא שכחתי Dt XXVI 13 (Maas Sh V 11)
שמעתי בקול ה' אלהי || עשיתי ככל אשר צויתני Dt XXVI 14 (Maas Sh V 12)
על כן לא יקמו רשעים במשפט || וחטאים בעדת צדיקים Ps I 5 (Snh X 3 R Nehemiah)
במדבר הזה יתמו || ושם ימתו Num XIV 35 (Snh X 3 R Aḳiba)
ותכס עליהם הארץ || ויאבדו מתוך הקהל Num XVI 33 (Snh X 3 R Aḳiba)
להנחיל אהבי יש || ואצרתיהם אמלא Pr VIII 21 (Ab V 19)

[39] E. g. R Eliezer in regard to Num XIV 35 and Num XVI 33 (Snh X 3) (However he objected to R Aḳiba's interpretation on historical-critical not text-critical grounds. Cf. the Mishnah).

[40] Cf. Bacher ibid. p. 98 for the sources and the meaning of this statement.

[41] E. g. בחריש וקציר Ex XXXIV 21 חריש=קציר in voluntary character (Shebi I 4 R Ishmael)

אניה בלב ים Pr XXX 19 ים=אניה in insusceptibility to uncleanliness (Sabb IX 2. Cf. the full interpretation in b 83b הא קמשמע לן מה ים טהור אף אניה טהורה)

היצר יחד לבם המבין אל כל מעשיהם Ps XXXIII 15 היצר=המבין in time (R Hash I 2)

ויעל משה ואהרן נדב ואביהו ושבעים מזקני ישראל Ex XXIV 9 שבעים מזקני ישראל= משה ואהרן נדב ואביהו in authority (R Hash II 9)

והרגת את האשה ואת הבהמה Lev XX 16 אשה=בהמה in manner of trial (Snh I 4)

ואיש . . . מות יומת ואת הבהמה תהרגו Lev XX 15 איש=בהמה in manner of trial (Snh I 4)

השור יסקל וגם בעליו יומת Ex XXI 29 בעליו=שור in manner of trial

שעיר עזים אחד חטאת מלבד חטאת הכפורים Num XXIX 11 חטאת כפורים=שעיר in atonement (Shebu I 3)

לא תאכלו כל נבלה . . . . . לא תבשל גדי בחלב אמו Dt XIV 21 נבלה=גדי in reference to species (Ḥull VIII 4 R Jose the Galilean)

על האפרחים או על הביצים Dt XXII 6 ביצים=אפרחים in characteristics (Ḥull XII 3)

(Malbim points to the fact that אפרחים and ביצים are needlessly repeated in this verse, whence the interpretation.)

והיה הוא ותמורתו Lev XXVII 10 הוא=תמורתו in incidence of sanctity (Tem I 1 R Aḳiba)

והיה הוא ותמורתו Lev XXVII 10 הוא=תמורתו in number (Tem I 2 R Simon)

Note: The affinity in the examples cited having the conjunction ו may have been indicated by the copulative character of this particle. Cf. the discussion of this point infra.

[42] Cf. Dobschütz p. 37 ff and infra

[43] E. g. Zech VI 14 in Midd III 8; Ez LXI 24 in Midd IV 1.

[44] Cf. Weiss ibid. I chapter 18 p. 158 ff and Dobschütz p. 48.

[45] לקט Lev IX 9 (Peah IV 10)
פרט Lev XIX 10 (Peah VII 3)
עוללות (תעולל) Lev XIX 10 (Peah VII 4)
דרך רחקה Num IX 10 (Pes IX 2)
קינה Jer IX 19 (M Ḳaṭ III 9)
מעות לא יוכל לתקן Eccl I 15 (Ḥag I 7)
פצוע דכה, כרות שפכה Dt XXIII 2 (Yab VIII 2)
נשך, תרבית Lev XXV 36 (B Meṣ V 1)
חרם Lev XXI 18 (Bekh VII 3)
טוב ברע Lev XXVII 10 (Tem I 2)
אתנן זונה, מחיר כלב Dt XXIII 19 (Tem VI 2 and 3)
שחין Lev XIII 18 (Neg IX 1)
מכוה Lev XIII 24 (Neg IX 1)
קרחת, גבחת Lev XIII 42 (Neg X 10)
טיט היון Ps XL 3 (Miḳw IX 2)

[46] המזבח אשר לפני ה' Lev XVI 18 (Yoma V 4)
אוב ידעוני Dt XVIII 11 (Snh VII 7)

[47] זונה Lev XXI 7 (Yab VI 5)
גבן Lev XXI 20 (Bekh VII 2)
מרוח אשך Lev XXI 20 (Bekh VII 5)
צרבת השחין Lev XIII 23 (Neg IX 2)

[48] הירא ורך הלבב Dt XX 8 (Soṭ VIII 5)
איתן Dt XXI 4 (Soṭ IX 5)

[49] קללת אלהים תלוי Dt XXI 23 (Snh VI 4)

[50] דמי אחיך Gen IV 10 (Snh IV 5)

[51] קטרות Ez XLVI 21 (Midd II 5)

[52] We distinguish the following classes:

A *Those instances in which the biblical source is explicitly referred to in the Mishnah in all the interpretations.*

(Note: Examples marked* are not textual exegesis. We cite the biblical and Mishnaic sources, the issue and the contending parties if any.)

They are:

Dt VI 7 construction of ובשכבך ובקומך (Ber I 3 Shammaiites vs Hillelites)
Dt XVI 3 meaning of כל ימי חייך (Ber I 5 B Zoma vs Sages)
Dt VI 5 meaning of ובכל מאדך (Ber IX 5 [4 in] 2 interpretations)
Ps CXIX 126 relation of עת לעשות לה' and הפרו תורתך (Ber IX 5 anon. vs R Nathan)

(Maimonides, basing himself on the statement of Raba b Ber 63a, holds that there is an exegetical difference between R Nathan and the anonymous author. Rashi on the other hand, believes that they agree.)

Dt XXIV 21 construction of כי (Peah VII 7 R Eliezer vs R Aḳiba)

Dt XXII 11 etymology of שעטנז (Kil IX 8 anon. vs R Simon b Elazar)

Ex XXXIV 21 implication of בחריש ובקציר תשבת (Shebi I 4 anon. vs R Ishmael)

Lev XXII 14 meaning of הקדש (Ter VI 6 R Eliezer vs R Aḳiba)

**Dt XXVI 15* reference of לנו (Maas Sh V 13–14 R Meir vs R Jose)

Gen XXXIV 25 implication of בהיותם כאבים (Sabb IX 3 anon. vs Sabb XIX R Elazar b Azariah)

Eccl I 15 meaning of מעות (Ḥag I 7 R Simon b Menasiah vs R Simon b Jochai)

Dt XXV 10 construction of בישראל (Yab XII 6 anon. vs R Judah)

I Sam I 11 meaning of מורה (Naz IX 5 R Nehorai vs R Jose)

Jud XIII 5 meanig of מורה (Naz IX 5 R Nehorai vs R Jose)

Num V 22 force of אמן אמן (Soṭ II 5 anon. vs R Meir)

Ex XV 1 meaning of לאמר (Soṭ V 4 R Aḳiba vs R Nehemiah)

Job XIII 15 meaning of לא (Soṭ V 5 R Joshua b Hyrḳanos vs Rabban Joḥanan b Zakkai)

Dt XXIV 1 meaning of דבר (anon. Soṭ VI 3 vs Shammaites and Hillelites Giṭṭ IX 10)

Dt XX 4 actual meaning of ה' אלהיכם ההלך עמכם (Soṭ VIII 1 two interpretations)

Dt XXIV 1 relation of ערות and דבר (Giṭṭ IX 10 Shammaiites vs Hillelites)

**Num XXXII 29–30* normativeness of the formula (Ḳidd III 4 R Meir vs R Ḥanina b Gamaliel)

Ex XXI 35 construction of המת (B Ḳam III 9 [The interpretation of Malbim is followed. Cf. infra] R Meir vs R Judah)

**II Sam III 31* normativeness of the king's conduct (Snh II 3 R Judah vs anon.)

Dt XVII 17 construction of ולא יסור לבבו. (Snh II 4 anon. vs R Judah vs R Simon)

Gen IV 10 construction of דמי (Snh IV 5 two interpretations)

Dt XXI 23 meaning of קללת אלהים תלוי (Snh VI 4 anon. [two in one] vs Snh VI 5 R Meir)

(O and PJ imply two different interpretations following our construction of the two interpretations implied in the Mishnah and designated by us as anonymous. Cf. infra.)

Dt XXI 20 force of זה (Snh VIII 4 two interpretations)

(The implication of two different interpretations of the same word in this Mishnah is noted in b Snh 71b)

II Chr XXXIII 13 construction of וישיבהו . . . למלכותו (Snh X 2 R Judah vs anon.)

Ps I 5 meaning of יקמו במשפט (Snh X 3 R Nehemiah vs anon.)

Dt XXIX 27 implication of כיום הזה (Snh X 3 R Aḳiba vs R Eliezer)

Dt XVII 17 meaning of עוד (Snh X 6 R Jose the Galilean vs R Aḳiba)

Dt XIX 21 implication of נפש בנפש (Makk I 6 Sadducees vs Sages)

Dt XVII 6 implication of על פי (Makk I 9 R Jose vs other interpretation)
Dt XIX 4 implication of דבר הרצח (Makk II 5 vs Makk II 8 || Shebi X 8)
Lev V 2 construction of ונעלם ממנו (Shebu II 5 R Eliezer vs R Aḳiba)
Cant I 2 vocalization of דדיך (Ab Zar II 5 R Ishmael vs R Joshua)
Lev VI 2 relation of על מוקדה and על המזבח (Zeb IX 1 R Joshua vs R Gamaliel)
Lev XXIV 7 meaning of על (Men XI 5 anon. vs Abba Saul)
Ex XXV 30 meaning of תמיד (Men XI 7 anon. vs R Jose)
Dt XIV 21 meaning of גדי (Ḥull VIII 4 R Aḳiba vs R Jose the Galilean)
Dt XXII 7 implication of שלח תשלח (Ḥull XII 3 two interpretations)
Lev XXVII 28 construction of קדש קדשים (Arakh VIII 6 R Judah b Bathyra
   vs Sages)
Lev XXV 27 implication of לאיש אשר (Arakh IX 2 two implications)
Lev XXV 33 relation of ערי and הלוים (Arakh IX 8 Rabbi vs Sages)
Lev XIX 20 implication of והפדה לא נפדתה (Ker II 5 R Aḳiba vs R Ishmael)
Lev XIII 30 meaning of דק (Neg XI R Aḳiba vs R Joḥanan b Nuri)
Lev XIV 29 relationship of לכפר (Neg XIV 10 R Aḳiba vs R Joḥanan b Nuri)
Gen I 10 meaning of ימים (Parah VIII 8 || Miḳw V 4 R Meir vs R Judah)
*Jer XLIX 6 implication of אחרי כן (Yad IV 4 R Gamaliel vs R Joshua)
B   *Those in which the biblical source is referred to only once but where there is
implied in the contrary opinion, that is quoted, a divergent interpretation which
is given in full in another Tannaitic source. They are:*
Lev XIX 10 meaning of וכרמך לא תעולל (Peah VII 6 R Eliezer vs R Aḳiba)
   Exegetical basis of controversy Sa: מכאן אמרו
*Is II 4 reprehensibility of the use of arms (Sabb VI 4 R Eliezer vs Sages)
   Exegetical basis of controversy Br b Sabb 63a and j
Gen V 2 function of ו in זכר ונקבה (Yab VI 6 Shammaiites vs Hillelites.) The
   exegetical basis of the controversy is clarified by the statement of R
   Nathan in the Tos Yab VIII 4, which is quoted in b 62a but reverses
   the authorities: ב"ש אומר זכר ונקבה ב"ה אומר או זכר או נקבה
Num V 26 implication of ואחר (Soṭ III 2 anon. vs R Simon). Exegetical basis
   is Se Num V 24 || b Soṭ 19b where R Simon is quoted to have interpreted
   לאחר כל המעשים כולן האמורין למעלה as ואחר ישקה. Cf. also Malbim ad loc.
Dt XXI 2 function of ו in זקניך ושפטיך (Soṭ IX 1 anon. vs R Judah). Exegetical
   basis of the controversy is Br b Soṭ 44b. That the issue is over the function of the ו is clear from both the b ibid. and the statement of j: מה מקיימין
   רבנין זקניך ושפטיך זקניך שהן שפטיך i. e. that is why R Simon, R Judah's opponent in the Br, does not count ושפטיך Cf. also Malbim ad loc.
Ex XXI 36 meaning of ישמרנו (B Ḳam IV 9 R Meir vs R Judah). Exegetical
   basis of the controversy is M
Lev XXI 12 meaning of מקדש (Snh II 1 R Meir vs R Judah). Exegetical basis
   of controversy Sa. b Snh 19a explains R Meir's construction of the clause
   ומקדושתו לא יצא as being ומן המקדש לא יצא

Num XVI 33 implication of ויאבדו (Snh X 3 R Aḳiba vs R Eliezer). Exegetical basis of the controversy Tos Snh XIII 9 where the view of R Eliezer is espoused by R Judah b Bathyra who interprets ויאבדו as denoting אבדה המתבקשת Cf. also Br b Snh 109b and j.

Dt XVII 13 meaning of ישמעו (Snh XI 4 R Aḳiba vs R Judah). Exegetical basis of the controversy Tos Snh XI 7 and MT || Br b Snh 89a: אמר ר' יהודה וכי נאמר יראו וייראו והלא לא נאמר אלא ישמעו וייראו

Dt XXV 2.3 construction of במספר. ארבעים (Makk III 10 anon. vs R Judah). Exegetical basis of the controversy Se. b Makk 22b explains the view of the anonymous author as follows: אי כתיב ארבעים במספר הוה אמינא ארבעים במניינא השתא דכתיב במספר ארבעים מניין שהוא סוכם את הארבעים
MT reflects no doubt the view of R Judah when it says: במספר שיהוא המכות במספר

Dt XIII 18 implication of מאומה (Ab Zar III 3 R Jose vs anon). Exegetical basis of the controversy Tos Ab Zar III (IV) 19, b 43b and j. Cf. also MT which quotes an opinion reflecting the view of the anonymous authors and Sifre which agrees with R Jose.

Lev XIV 21 relationship of ולג שמן (Men IX 3 anon. vs R Eliezer b Jacob). Exegetical basis of the controversy Sa || b Men 89a

Lev XXVII 22 meaning of משדה אחוזתו (Arakh VII 5 R Meir vs R Judah vs R Simon). Exegetical basis of controversy Sa || b Arakh 26b

Lev XXVII 26 implication of לא יקדיש (Arakh VIII 7 anon. vs R Ishmael). Exegetical basis of controversy Sa.

Lev XXV 30 meaning of שנה תמימה (Arakh IX 3 anon. vs Rabbi). Exegetical basis of controversy Sa || Br b 31 b.

Lev IV 23 emphasis in אשר חטא בה (Ker IV 3 R Joshua vs R Eliezer). Exegetical basis of controversy Sa.

Lev XIV 36 construction of ... ולא יטמא (Neg XII 5 R Judah vs R Simon). Exegetical basis of controversy Sa. Cf. Malbim.

Num VIII 8 meaning of שני (Parah I 2 R Jose the Galilean vs Sages). Exegetical basis of controversy Tos Parah I 1: אמרו לו איני אומר שני אלא שני לראשון

Dt XXIII 19 implication of בית ה' אלהיך (Parah II 3 anon. vs R Eliezer). Exegetical basis of controversy Se: בית ה' אלהיך פרט לפרת חטאת שאינה באה לבית דברי ר' אליעזר וחכמים אומרים לרבות את הריקועים MT's statement: בית ה' אלהיך אינו חייב על הבאתו עד שיביאו לשם זבח אבל לבדק הבית מותרין no doubt reflects the view of the anonymous author.

C *Those in which only one interpretation is explicitly recorded in the Mishnah of a passage to which more or other interpretations are given elsewhere in Tannaitic sources.*

Dt VI 7 meaning of בדרך (Ber I 3 Hillelites). Other interpretation Br b Ber 11a

Ex XII 28 meaning of תאחר (Ter III 6 anon.). This and other interpretation in MS in name of R Eliezer

Dt XXVI 14 meaning of למת (Maas Sh V 12 anon.) This and other interpretation in Sa in name of R Aḳiba.

Lev XVI 6 meaning of ביתו (Yoma I 1 R Judah). Other interpretation in Sa Lev XVI 15 for ביתו of Lev XVI 11

Num XXX 10 meaning of ונדר אלמנה וגרושה כל אשר אסרה על נפשה (Ned XI 9 anon.) Tos Ned VII 6, b Ned 89a and j cite controversy between R Aḳiba and R Ishmael

Job I 1 implication of ירא אלהים (Soṭ V 5 Rabban Joḥanan b Zakkai) . Divergent interpretation in name of R Meir in Br b Soṭ 31a

Jos VIII 33 construction of ונגד הכהנים הלוים (Soṭ *VII* 3 anon.) This and divergent interpretation in name of R Simon in Br j.

Dt XX 6 meaning of כרם (Soṭ VIII 2 anon.) This and other interpretation in name of R Eliezer Tos Soṭ VII 18 || Se R Eliezer b Jacob.

Dt XXIV 15 reference of שכרו (B Meṣ IX 12 anon.) This and divergent interpretation of R Jose b R Judah Br b B Meṣ 111b R Ḥananiah ibid.

Lev XIX 13 reference of פעלת שכיר (B Mṣ IX 12 anon.) This and divergent view of R Jose b R Judah in Br b B Meṣ 111b.

Dt XXIV 17 meaning of בגד אלמנה (B Meṣ IX 13 anon.) This and divergent interpretation in name of R Simon in Tos B Meṣ X 10 || Br b B Meṣ 115a and j.

Gen VI 3 meaning of ידון רוחי באדם לעלם (Snh X 3 anon.) This and other interpretation in Tosephtah Snh XIII 6 || Br b Snh 108a and j.

Dt XIII 14 etymology of בליעל (Snh X 4 anon.) Other etymology Se || Br b 111b.

Dt XIII 17 implication of רחבה (Snh X 6 anon.) || Se in name of R Aḳiba). This and divergent interpretation in name of R Ishmael in Br b Snh 112a

Dt XIX 3 meaning of תכין . . . הדרך (Makk II 5 anon.) This and divergent interpretation in MT || Br b Makk 10a and j

Dt XXV 3 meaning of ונקלה (Makk III 15 anon.) This and divergent interpretations in Se and Br b Makk 23a

**Lev VII 33* strictness of the application of המקריב את דם השלמים ואת החלב (Zeb XII 1 anon.) This and divergent interpretation in name of Abba Saul in Sa.

Lev XXII 28 meaning of יום אחד (Ḥull V 5 anon.) This and divergent interpretation in name of R Meir in Sa

D *Those in which only one express interpretation of a passage is given in both the Mishnah and other Tannaitic sources but another is implied by the opinion diverging from the one based on the exegesis. They are, taking first those that have been recognized by the Amoraim*:

Ps LXVII 27 construction of במקהלות (Ber VII 3 R Jose the Galilean). Implied interpretation of R Aḳiba discussed by j: בכל קהלה וקהלה

**Is XXX 14* which is to be used as proof לחשוף מים מגבא or לחתות אש מיקוד (Sabb VIII 7). Two exclusive views of R Meir and R Jose discussed b Sabb 82a

Lev VI 16 emphasis in כל מנחת כהן (Shek I 4 Priests according to Rabban Joḥanan b Zakkai). Other interpretation is implied. Cf. discussion in j: כן משיבין חכמים לרבי יהודה . . . מנחת יחיד קריבה כליל ואין מנחת הצבור קריבה כליל

Ex XXVI 33 construction of הפרכת (Yoma V 1 R Jose). The exegetical reason for the divergent view of the anonymous author is suggested in both b Yoma 51b and j.

Jos VI 5 meaning of שופר (R Hash III 2 R Jose). The exegetical reason for the divergent view of the anonymous author is suggested in both b R Hash 26a and j.

Ex XXIII 14 implication of רגלים (Ḥag I 1 Hillelites). According to j the divergent view of the Shammaiites is based on the exegesis of the same passages as that of the Hillelites ב"ה וב"ש מקרא אחד הן דורשין

Gen I 28 addressees in פרו ורבו (Yab VI 6 R Joḥanan b Baroḳa). The exegetical reason for the divergent view of the anonymous author is suggested in both b Yab 65b and j.

Num XXX 14 relationship of אישה יקימנו and אישה יפירנו (Ned X 7 Sages). The reason for the divergent view of R Eliezer is implied in the statement of b Ned 76b: בעלמא דרשי קל וחומר ושאני הכא דאמר קרא אישה . . . ואישה

Num V 29 implication of ו in ונטמאה (Soṭ V 1 R Aḳiba). b Soṭ 28a gives as the exegetical reason for R Aḳiba's interpretation that רבי עקיבא ו"וי קדריש whereas Rabbi does not.

Lev XI 33 force of יטמא (Soṭ V 2 R Aḳiba). According to j Pes I halakha 7 the opponents of R Aḳiba base their view on Num XIX 15 . . . וכל כלי פתוח טמא הוא i. e. טמא הוא ואינו נעשה אב הטומאה

Dt XXV 9 meaning of וענתה (Soṭ VII 3 anon.) The exegetical reason for the divergent interpretation of R Judah is suggested by b Soṭ 33a ff.

Dt XXV 9 construction of ככה (Soṭ VII 3 R Judah). The exegetical reason for the divergent interpretation of the anon. author is suggested by b Soṭ 33b

Dt XXIV 1 construction of כי (Giṭṭ IX 10 R Aḳiba). The exegetical reason for the divergent views of the Shammaiites and the Hillelites is suggested in b Giṭṭ 90a: במאי קמיפלגי בדר"ל דאמר ר"ל כי משמע בד' לשונות

Num XI 16 meaning of עמך (Snh I 6 anon.) The exegetical reason for the divergent view of R Judah is implied in b Snh 16b: מאי טעמא דרבנן דאמרי ומשה על גביהן אמר קרא התיצבו שם עמך עמך ואת בהדייהו ורבי יהודה עמך משום שכינה

Lev XXIII 14 meaning of עד (Men X 5 R Judah). The exegetical reason for the divergent view of Rabban Joḥanan b Zakkai is given in j Ḥallah I halakha 1: א"ר הילא טעמא דר' יוחנן עד עצם היום הזה מלמד שהיום מתיר b Men 68b (Rab Nachman bar Isaac) makes it clear that the meaning of עד is the issue.

Is VII 21 meaning of צאן (Ḥull XI 2 Shammaiites). The exegetical basis for their view and that of their opponents the Hillelites who stress I Sam XXV 18 is suggested in b Ḥull 137a.

Lev XXV 34 implication of ושדה מגרש עריהם לא ימכר כי אחזת עולם הוא להם (Arakh VIII 5 Rabbi). The exegetical reason for the divergent view of R Judah is suggested in b Arakh 28a.

Lev XXVII 10 construction of ותמורתו (Tem I 2 R Simon b Elazar). The exegetical reason for the divergent view of the anonymous author is suggested in b Tem 9a.

Joel II 23 meaning of בראשון (Taan I 2 R Meir. His opponent is R Judah).

Num VI 12 construction of ימים (Naz III 5 R Eliezer). For implied view of anonymous author cf. Malbim.

Ex XXII 5 relationship of את הבערה (B Ḳam VI 4 R Simon. His opponents are R Elazar b Azariah, R Eliezer and R Aḳiba).

**Num V 13 and 27* force of repetition of נטמאה (Soṭ V 1 Rabbi. His opponent in exegesis is R Aḳiba who stresses other feature).

Lev IX 22 meaning of וישא . . . אל (Soṭ VII 6 R Judah. His opponent is anon.)

**Ex XXII 7* construction of . . . אם (B Meṣ III 12 Hillelites. Their opponents are the Shammaittes who stress another verse. Cf. M and MS || Br b B Meṣ 43b and Br j).

**II Sam XII 8* normativeness of ואתנה לך . . . את נשי אדניך בחיקך (Snh II 2 R Judah. His opponent is the anonymous author).

Num XIV 35 implication of ושם ימתו (Snh X 3 R Aḳiba. The Tos Snh XIII 10 expresses the divergent view of his opponent R Eliezer, who stresses another verse, more clearly: . . . .הן באין לעולם הבא שנאמר אספו לי חסידי).

**Dt XXIV 7* construction of והתעמר (Snh XI 1 R Judah. His opponent the anonymous author stresses . . . ונמצא בידו Ex XXI 17. Cf. M).

Lev XIX 28 construction of אני ה' (Makk III 6 R Simon b Judah. His opponent is the anonymous author).

**Lev V 2 and 3* force of repetition of ונעלם (Shebu II 5 R Ishmael. His opponents are R Eliezer and R Aḳiba who stress only verse 2).

Is LXVI 23 meaning of והיה מדי שבת בשבתו (Ed II 10 R Joḥanan ben Nuri. His opponent the anonymous author stresses the earlier part of the verse והיה מדי חדש בחדשו Cf. ibid).

Dt VII 26 implication of שקץ תשקצנו (Ab Zar III 6 anon. His opponent R Aḳiba stresses Is XXX 22).

Is XXX 22 implication of תזרם כמו דוה (Sabb IX 1 || Ab Zar III 6 R Aḳiba. His opponent the anonymous author stresses Dt VII 26).

Lev XXIV 5 implication of ואפית (Men VI R Simon. His opponent is the anonymous author).

Ex XIII 12 construction of הזכרים (Bekh II 6 R Jose the Galilean. His opponents are the Sages).

Ex XIII 2 relationship of בבני ישראל (Bekh VIII 1 R Jose the Galilean. His opponent is the anonymous author).

Lev XXVII 10 relationship of הוא and ותמורתו (Tem I 1 R Aḳiba. His opponent is R Joḥanan ben Nuri. He is unable to refute R Aḳiba's exegesis according to Sa).

Num XV 29 meaning of לעושה (Ker I 2 Sages. Their opponent is R Meir).

Ez XLI 24 explanation of the construction of the edifice (Midd IV 1 R Judah. His opponent is the anonymous author).

Lev XI 38 implication of יתן (Makhsh I 3 Hillelites. Their opponents are the Shammaiites).

[53] I chapter 18 p. 158 ff.

[54] Conclusive evidence are the following remarks of the Tannaim themselves:

Ter VI 6: ממקום שרבי אליעזר מיקל משם רבי עקיבא מחמיר

Maas Sh V 14: מכאן אמרו referring to Dt XXVI 15

B Ḳam III 9: קיימת. ומכרו את השור החי וחצו את כספו" ולא קיימת. וגם את המת יחצון" referring to Ex XXI 35.

[55] Ber IX 5: Ruth II 4

Ber IX 5: Jud VI 12
Peah V 6: Pr XXII 28
Peah VII 3: Pr XXII 28
Sheḳ I 5: Ezra IV 3
Sheḳ III 3: Num XXXII 22
Sheḳ III 3: Pr III 4
Yoma VIII 9: Ez XXXVI 25
Sukk II 6: Eccl I 15
R Hash II 9: Ex XXIV 9
Taan I 7: I Sam XII 17
Taan III 3: Amos IV 7
Taan III 8: Pr XXIII 25
Ḥag I 6: Eccl I 15
Ned III 11: Jer IX 25
Soṭ I 6: Ez XXIII 48
Soṭ I 8: Jud XVI 21
Soṭ I 8: II Sam XVIII 15
Soṭ I 8: II Sam XV 6
Soṭ I 8: II Sam XVIII 14
Soṭ I 9: Ex II 4
Soṭ I 9: Num XII 15
Soṭ I 9: Gen L 7
Soṭ I 9: Ex XIII 19
Soṭ I 9: Dt XXXIV 6
Soṭ VIII 1: II Chr XXVIII 15
Soṭ VIII 6: I Sam IV 17
Soṭ VIII 6: I Sam XXXI 1
Soṭ IX 9: Micah VII 1.2
Ḳidd I 10: Eccl IV 12
Ḳidd IV 14: Gen XXIV 1
B Ḳam VIII 1: Dt XXV 11
B Ḳam VIII 7: Gen XX 7
B Ḳam VIII 7: Gen XX 17
B Ḳam IX 7: Lev V 21.22
Snh IV 5: Pr XI 10
Snh IV 5: Lev V 1
Snh VI 1: Lev XXIV 14
Snh VI 2: Jos VII 19.20
Snh X 3: I Sam II 6
Snh X 6: Dt XIII 18
Snh XI 2: Dt XVII 10
Makk II 4: Num XXXV 14
Makk III 15: Lev XVIII 29
Makk III 15: Lev XVIII 5.6
Makk III 15: Dt XII 23.24.25
Ed VIII 7: Mal III 23.24
Ab II 9: Ps XXXVII 21
Ab III 2: Ez XLI 22
Ab III 7: I Chr XXIX 14
Ab IV 1: I Sam II 30
Ab IV 1: Pr XVI 32
Ab V 4: Num XIV 22
Ab V 18: I Kings XV 30
Ab V 19: Ps LV 24
Zeb X 1: Num XXVIII 23
Men XIII 10: II Kings XXIII 9
Bekh IV 1: Dt XV 20
Neg XII 2: Lev XIV 35
Yad IV 4: Is X 13
Yad IV 7: Ex V 2
Yad IV 7: Ex IX 27
Uḳṣ III 12: Ps XXIX 11

[56] Ber IX 5: Dt VI 5

Ber IX 5: Pr XXIII 22
Peah VIII 9: Ex XXIII 8
Peah VIII 9: Dt XVI 20
Shebi X 3: Dt XV 9
Maas Sh V 10.11.12.13: Dt XXVI 13.14.15
Sabb IX 2: Pr XXX 19
Sabb IX 2: Is LXI 11

Sabb IX 3: Ex XIX 15
Sabb IX 3: Is I 18
Sabb IX 4: Ps CIX 18
Sabb IX 6: Dt XIII 18
Pes V 3: Lev XXIII 5
Pes X 5: Ex XIII 8
Sheḳ VI 6: Lev V 19
Yoma VI 8: Is I 18
R Hash I 2: Ps XXXIII 15
R Hash III 8: Ex XVII 11
R Hash III 8: Num XXI 8
Taan IV 2: Num XXVIII 2
Taan IV 8: Cant III 11
Meg III 3: Lev XXVI 31
M Ḳaṭ III 9: Is XXV 8
Yab IX 6: Lev XXII 13
Yab XII 6: Dt XXV 8
Yab XII 6: Dt XXV 9
Naz IX 5: I Sam XVI 2
Soṭ II 2: Num V 17
Soṭ II 4: Num V 23
Soṭ V 1: Num V 22 and 24
Soṭ V 3: Num XXXV 4 and 5
Soṭ V 5: Job XXVII 5
Soṭ VIII 1: Dt XX 3
Soṭ VIII 2: Dt XX 5.6.7
Soṭ VIII 4: Dt XXIV 5
Soṭ IX 6: Dt XXI 7
Soṭ IX 11: Is XXIV 9
Soṭ IX 12: Ps XII 2
Ḳidd IV 12: Ps XCII 15
Ḳidd IV 14: Is XL 31
B Ḳam IX 12: Num V 10
B Meṣ IX 13: Dt XXIV 6
B Meṣ IX 13: Dt XXIV 11
Snh I 4: Lev XX 15 and 16
Snh I 4: Ex XXI 29
Snh II 4: Dt XVII 17
Snh II 4: Dt XVII 19
Snh VI 4: Dt XVII 7
Snh VIII 4: Dt XXI 19 and 20
Snh X 3: Gen XI 8 and 9
Snh X 3: Gen XIII 13
Snh X 3: Num XIV 37
Snh X 3: Ps L 5
Snh X 5: Dt XIII 16
Snh XI 5: Dt XVIII 19
Makk I 6: Dt XIX 19
Makk II 6: Num XXXV 25
Shebu I 3: Num XXIX 11
Ed II 9: Gen XV 13 and 16
Ab II 13: Joel II 13
Ab III 2: Ps I 1.2
Ab III 2: Mal III 6
Ab III 6: Ex XX 24
Ab III 6: Mal III 16
Ab III 17: Jer XVII 6
Ab III 17: Jer XVII 8
Ab IV 1: Ps CXXVIII 2
Ab V 19: Pr VIII 21
Hor III 3: Lev IV 22
Zeb IX 5: Lev I 9
Zeb XIV 1: Lev XVII 4
Ḥull II 3: Dt XXVII 7
Ḥull VIII 4: Dt XIV 21
Ḥull XI 2: Dt XVIII 4
Ḥull XII 3: Dt XXII 6 על האפרחים או על הביצים
Bekh I 7: Ex XIII 13
Bekh I 7: Ex XXI 8
Bekh I 7: Lev XXVII 27
Arakh III 5: Num XIV 22
Ker VI 9: Lev IV 32
Ker VI 9: Lev XII 6
Ker VI 9: Lev XIX 3
Midd II 5: Ez XLVI 21.22
Midd III 8: Zech VI 14
Neg XII 6: Lev XIV 38
Yad IV 4: Amos IX 14
Uḳṣ III 12: Pr VIII 21

[57] We use the term examples of literal exegesis in a broad sense including those instances in which the exegesis is only implied in the use made of the verse.

Pr XI 27 meaning of רעה (Peah VIII 9)
Jer XVII 7 meaning of ברוך, יבטח, מבטחו (Peah VIII 9)

Ex XXII 28 meaning of מלאתך, דמעך (Ter III 6. The exegesis which is only implied in the Mishnah is expressly given in MS)
Dt XXVI 14 meaning of באני (Maas Sh V 12)
Dt XXVI 14 construction of בטמא (Maas Sh V 12). The construction is more explicitly defined in Sifre
Ex XXIII 19 force of ך in אדמתך (Bik I 2)
Ex XXIII 16 construction of בכורי מעשיך (Bik I 3)
Ex XXIII 19 construction of בית ה' אלהיך (Bik I 9)
Ex XIII 7 construction of לך (Pes II 2)
Ex XII 6 construction of כל קהל עדת ישראל (Pes V 5)
Lev XVI 30 relationship of לפני ה' (Yoma VIII 9)
Jer XIV 8 etymology of מקוה (Yoma VIII 9)
Lev XXIII 4 meaning of תקראו (R Hash I 9)
Lev XXIII 4 force of אתם (R Hash II 9) Br b R Hash 25a gives full exegesis. Cf. note 36
Lev XXIII 44 meaning of וידבר (Meg III 6)
Jer IX 19 meaning of קינה (M Ḳaṭ III 9)
Dt XVI 17 construction of . . . כ . . . כ (Ḥag I 5)
Dt XXV 5 force of אחד (Yab III 9)
Dt XXIII 2 meaning of יבא . . . בקהל ה' (Yab VIII 2)
Lev XXI 7 meaning of מאישה (Yab X 3)
Dt XXV 8 construction of . . . וקראו (Yab XII 6)
Ex XXI 22 meanings of ענוש יענש, אסון (Ket III 2)
Dt XXII 29 construction of ולו תהיה לאשה (Ket III 5)
Jer IX 25 meaning of ערלים (Ned III 11)
I Sam XVII 36 meaning of הערל (Ned III 11)
II Sam I 20 meaning of הערלים (Ned III 11)
Jer XXXIII 25 meaning of בריתי (Ned III 11. b Ned 32a quotes a divergent interpretation by the Amora R Elazar).
Is LVIII 8 construction of . . . והלך meaning of יאספך (Soṭ I 9)
Num V 23 meaning of ספר (Soṭ II 4)
Num V 13 meaning of עד (Soṭ VI 3 The exegesis is more explicit in Se || b Soṭ 31b)
Dt XXVI 5 meaning of ועניית (Soṭ VII 3. The theory underlying this interpretation is found in b Soṭ 33b. It is refuted in j)
Dt XXVII 14 meaning of וענו (Soṭ VII 3 and 4. b Soṭ 33a and j ad loc. give origin of this interpretation).
Dt XI 30 identification of אלוני מרה (Soṭ VII 5. According to Se || Mt || Br b Soṭ 33b || j the Samaritans inserted שכם after אלוני מרה)
Dt XXVII 8 meaning of באר (Soṭ VII 5)
Dt XXXI 10 meanings of מקץ, מעד (Soṭ VII 8).
Dt XX 2 force of ה in הכהן, meaning of ודבר (Soṭ VIII 1)
Dt XXI 1 meanings of באדמה, נפל, בשדה (Soṭ IX 2)
Dt XXI 8 division of discourse (Soṭ IX 6)
Hosea IV 14 meaning of אפקד (Soṭ IX 9)

Dt XXIV 1 force of לה (Giṭṭ III 2)
Is XLV 18 meaning of לשבת (Giṭṭ IV 5 || Ed I 13)
Gen XXVI 5 meaning of תורתי (Ḳidd IV 14. The exegesis is more explicit in Tos Ḳidd V 21)
Ex XXI 35 meaning of רעהו (B Ḳam IV 3)
Ex XXI 28 meaning of יגח (B Ḳam IV 4)
Ex XXII 5 meaning of השדה (B Ḳam VI 4. The exegesis is more explicit in M. Cf. also b B Ḳam 60a)
Ex XXI 37 emphasis in תחת השור . . . תחת השה (B Ḳam VII 1)
Num V 8 meaning of האשם המושב and construction of לה' לכהן (B Ḳam IX 11. The exegesis is much more explicit in Se and SZ and Brs b B Ḳam 110a)
Num V 10 force of לו (B Ḳam IX 12)
Dt XXII 2 construction of אחיך (B Meṣ II 7)
Dt XXII 2 construction of והשבותו (B Meṣ II 7)
Dt XXII 1 force of השב (B Meṣ II 9. The Amora Raba expatiates on the matter in b B Meṣ 31a)
Ex XXIII 5 force of עזב (B Meṣ II 10)
Ex XXIII 5 meaning of עמו (B Meṣ II 10)
Ex XXII 20 meanings of גר, הונה (B Meṣ IV 10)
Num XIV 27 meaning of עדה (Snh I 6. j gives other biblical source).
Ex XXIII 2 meanings of רבים, לרעת, להטת and construction of אחרי רבים להטת (Snh I 6)
Num XXXV 24.25 meanings of ושפטו, העדה, והצילו (Snh I 6)
Dt XVII 15 meaning of עליך (Snh II 5)
Lev XIX 16 meaning of עמיך (Snh III 7)
Lev XXIV 22 meaning of משפט and relationship of משפט אחד יהיה לכם (Snh IV 1)
Jos VII 25 force of הזה (Snh VI 2)
Dt XXI 18 meaning of בן (Snh VIII 1)
Dt XXI 20 meaning and construction of זולל, סבא (Snh VIII 2)
Is LX 21 meaning of לעלם, ארץ (Snh X 1)
Dt XXIX 27 construction of כיום הזה (Snh X 3. The same construction is implied in remark of Tos Snh XIII 12 || Br b Snh 110b and j: אם מעשיהן כיום הזה הם באין ואם לאו אינן באין)
Dt XIII 17 force of ה in שללה (Snh X 6)
Dt XIII 17 meaning of כליל (Snh X 6)
Dt XXIV 7 meaning of והתעמר (Snh XI 1. Midrash Tannaim explicitly gives meaning of והתעמר)
Dt XVII 12 meaning of יעשה (Snh XI 2. The exegesis is clearer in Se, MT and Brs b Snh 88b and j).
Dt XIX 5 construction of ואשר . . . (Makk II 2)
Num XXXV 13 meaning of תהיינה (Makk II 4)
Dt XXV 2 meaning of והפילו (Makk III 13)
Dt XXV 3 construction of ונקלה אחיך לעיניך (Makk III 15)
Is XLII 21 meaning of יגדיל (Makk III 16)
Lev V 4 force of להרע and להיטיב (Shebu III 5)

Is XLI 4 meaning and construction of מראש (Ed II 9)
Dt VII 26 meaning of תועבה (Ab Zar I 9)
Dt VII 25 relationship of עליהם (Ab Zar III 5)
Dt XII 2 relationship of על ההרים, על הגבעות (Ab Zar III 5)
Lam III 28 meaning of כי נטל (Ab III 2)
Is XXVIII 8 meaning of מקום (Ab III 3)
Ps LXXXII 1 meaning of עדת (Ab III 6)
Amos IX 6 meaning of אגדתו (Ab III 6)
Ps LXXXII 1 meaning of אלהים 2 (Ab III 6)
Dt IV 9 meaning of נפשך and הדברים (Ab III 8)
Pr IV 2 meaning of תורתי (Ab III 14)
Ps CXIX 99 meaning of מכל . . . השכלתי (Ab IV 1)
Ps CXXVIII 2 construction of כי (Ab IV 1)
Ps CXXVIII 2 etymology of אשריך (Ab IV 1)
Dt XXXIII 21 meanings of חלקת, מחקק (Ab V 18. The exegesis is more explicit in Tos Soṭ IV 8.9, MT and Se where all the difficulties are discussed).
Lev IV 13 meaning of עדת (Hor I 4)
Lev IV 13 meaning of נעלם and דבר (Hor I 3)
Lev VI 2 meaning of העלה (Zeb IX 1)
Dt XII 27 construction of הבשר והדם (Zeb IX 5)
Lev II 11 meaning of כל (Men V 2)
Ex XXIX 27 meaning of הורם, הונף (Men V 6)
Lev VII 14 meaning of אחד (Men VII 2)
Lev VII 12 emphasis on התודה (Men VII 4)
Dt XVI 2 construction of צאן ובקר (Men VII 6)
Lev XXIV 2 relationship of למאור (Men VIII 5)
Num XXVIII 20 relationship of ומנחתם (Men VIII 7)
Num XXVIII 31 construction of ונסכיהם (Men VIII 7)
Ex XXV 30 vocalization of פנים (Men XI 4)
Num II 20 meaning of על (Men XI 5)
Gen I 5 construction of יום אחד (Ḥull V 5)
Lev VII 34 force of אתם (Ḥull X 1)
Dt XXII 6 construction of ביצים, אפרחים, קן צפור (Ḥull XII 3)
Dt XXII 7 force of שלח (Ḥull XII 3)
Ex XIII 13 construction of פטר חמור (Bekh I 2)
Ex XXXIV 20 construction of פטר חמור (Bekh I 2)
Ex XXXIV 20 meaning of שה (Bekh I 4)
Num XVIII 15 force of פדה (Bekh XIII 9)
Lev XXVII 32 meaning of צאן (Bekh IX 1)
Lev XXVII 7 meaning of מבן ששים שנה ומעלה (Arakh IV 4)
Lev I 3 meaning of לרצנו (Arakh V 6)
Lev XXVII 21 relationship of כשדה החרם (Arakh VIII 6)
Lev XXV 15 force of שני (Arakh IX 1)
Lev XXV 30 meaning of לצמיתת (Arakh IX 4)

Lev XXVII 10 force of יחליפנו, ימיר (Tem I 6)
Dt XXIII 19 force of גם שניהם (Tem VI 2)
Lev IV 28 force of ו in חטאתו (Ker VI 7)
Ez XLI 23 construction of שתים דלתות (Midd IV 1)
Is XXIX 1 etymology of אריאל (Midd IV 7)
Lev XIII 12 meaning of לכל מראה (Neg II 3)
Lev XIV 42 force of ולקחו, והביאו, יקח, וטח (Neg XII 6)
Lev XIV 53 meaning of אל פני (Neg XIV 2)
Ex XXI 21 meaning of יום, או, יומים (Zab II 3)
Lev XI 38 meaning of יתן (Makhsh I 3)
Ps XXV 14 meaning of סוד (Yad IV 3)

NOTES II

[1] R. Aḳiba's interpretation of Lev XXII 4 (R Hash II 9) is based not on the vocalization of אתָם as אַתֶּם but rather, as Br b R Hash 25a indicates, on the threefold occurrence of that word in the context. The same Tanna's ascription to יִטְמָא Lev XI 33 (Soṭ V 2) of an active meaning does not necessarily prove that he read יְטַמֵּא. It is more likely, as the remark in j Pes chapter I halakha 7 וכל כלי פתוח... טמא הוא (במדבר י"ט ט"ו) הוא טמא ואינו נעשה אב הטומאה seems to imply, that he derived the support for his view from the difference in significance between the imperfect and the participle intimating that the former denotes action and the latter state. Cf. Malbim hereon.

[2] The reading of פָּנִים Ex XXV 30 by R Eliezer (Men XI 4) as פַּנִּים was meant merely as an aid to the memory, just like his colleague R Judah's mnemonic זד"ד יה"ן, for as far as the halakha is concerned there is no difference of opinion between them. Cf. Tossafoth Yomṭob ad loc.

[3] Cf. Abraham Geiger, Urschrift und Übersetzungen der Bibel in ihrer Abhängigkeit von der innern Entwickelung des Judenthums, Breslau 1857, p. 410 ff. with reference to the debate of R Joshua and R Ishmael (Ab Zar II 5) over the vocalization of דדיך Cant I 2.

[4] Dt XXII 11.

[5] Kil IX 8 anon.

[6] Cf. Dobschütz p. 27.

[7] E. g. מורה I Sam I 11 = מורא (R. Jose Naz IX 5). The translation of J ומרות אנש indicates the possibility that what R Jose meant was not "fear" but "lordship". However the citation in this connection by R Jannai in j of Is VII 25, in which the word יראת occurs, proves that the Palestinian Amoraim, at least, interpreted R Jose's construction of the word as ⇄ מורא "fear").

[8] לא Job XIII 15 ⇄ לו (R Joshua b Hyrḳanos Soṭ V 5. Cf. also the remark of b Soṭ 31a that לא may stand for the negative לא as well as the preposition with the pronominal suffix, i. e. לוֹ).

[9] פ"א = פ"נ e.g. א[פה] (אפית Lev XXIV 5) = נ[פה] (עד שתהא מ נ ו פ ה Men VI 7 R Simon)

ע'ו פ'א=ל'ה פ'ו e. g. [ד]או (מאדך Dt VI 5)=י[ד]ה (הוי מ ו ד ה לו) Ber IX 5 part of second interpretation. That this remark is also intended as interpretation of מאדך is evident from Se: הוי מודה לו כיעקב. מ is not taken to be part of the root here and the form מאד must have been conceived as analogous to מָקוֹם from קום or מָאוֹר from אוֹר)

ע'א=ע'ע e. g. [ד]א[מ] (מאדך Dt VI 5)=ד[מד] (בכל מ ד ה ו מ ד ה שהוא מודד לך Ber IX 5 part of second interpretation. MT says distinctly: בכל מאד ומאד i. e. מְאֹד may be merely another orthography for מוֹד, infinitive construct of מדד. Cf. Reifmann, Beth Talmud, Vienna 1881, I p. 379)

ע'ו=ע'י e. g. [ן]ו[ד] (ידון Gen VI 3)=[ן]י[ד] (ד י ן Snh VI 3)

ע'ע=ל'ה e. g. ם[עמ] (עמיך Lev XIX 16)=ה[עמ] (ח ב ר י Snh III 7=עמיתך as in Lev XIX 15 and 17?)

ל"ה=ע'ע e. g. ה[אנ] (אני Dt XXVI 14)=ן[אנ] (א נ י נ ה Maas Sh V 12)

ל"ן=ע"ע e. g. ן[גב] (גבן Lev XXI 20)=ב[גב] (שיש לו שני ג ב י ם Bekh VII 2 R Ḥanina b Antigonos)

ל"א=ל"ה Cf. מורה note 7.

[10] אשר (אשריך Ps CXXVIII 2)=עשר (איזהו עשיר Ab IV 1).

[11] Playing on the last two letters of שעטנז (Dt XXII 11) which was broken up (Kil IX 8) into שע+ט+נז R Simon b Elazar says נלוז ומליז i. e. לז=נז according to him.

[12] E. g. אשך [מ]רוח (Lev XXI 20)=כל ש[רוח] באשכיו (Bekh VII 5 R Akiba). Cf. also מאדך note 9.

[13] Cf. שעטנז notes 4 and 5 and

בליעל (Dt XIII 14)=בלי+יעל or בלי+על (אין להם חלק לעולם הבא Snh X 4⇐ עדת קורח אינה עתידה ל ע ל ו ת Snh X 3)

א ר י א ל (Is XXIX 1)=ארי+על (ודומה ל א ר י Midd IV 7).

[14] Cf. Dobschütz p. 27.

[15] Cf. also Dobschütz p. 32.

[16] E. g. מורה which occurs only in Jud XIII 5, XVI 17 and I Sam I 11=מורא (R Jose Naz IX 5) "fear" which in Ps IX 21 actually has the spelling מורה.

ידון (Gen VI 3), which S treats as a hapaxlegomenon and translates καταμείνῃ=from דין (Snh VI 3) "judge" as e. g. in Gen XLIX 16.

שעטנז (cf. notes 4 and 5 above) which occurs only in Lev XIX 19 and Dt XXII 11.

[17] E. g. ק¹ל²ה (נקלה Dt XXV 3)=the neo-Hebrew ל²ק¹ה (כשלקה Makk III 15 R Ḥananiah b Gamaliel)

[18] E. g. מרוח¹ א²שך (Lev XXI 20) which is a hapaxlegomenon מרא²ה ח¹שך (שמראיו חשוכין Bekh VII 5 R Ḥanina b Antigonos).

[19] E. g. מקוה (Jer XIV 8) "hope"=מקוה "gathering (of water)" (Yoma VIII 9 R Akiba) as e. g. in Gen I 10.

[20] Ter III 6 commenting on Ex XXII 28 לא תאחר. Cf. also discussion of Meklenburg, הכתב והקבלה ad loc.

[21] Shebi X 8 commenting on Dt XV 2 דבר השמטה, Shebi X 8 || Makk II 8 commenting on Dt XIX 9 דבר הרצח. Cf. Malbim ad loc.

[22] Makk II 5 commenting on Dt XIX 3 תכין לך הדרך. Cf. also Meklenburg הכתב הקבלה ad loc.

[23] Men V 6 commenting on Ex XXIX 27 אשר הונף ואשר הורם.

[24] Makk I 9 commenting on Dt XVII 6 על פי שנים עדים.

[25] Soṭ VII 3 commenting on Dt XXVI 5 וענית ואמרת.
Soṭ VII 3.4 commenting on Dt XXVII 14 וענו ואמרו
Soṭ VII 4 commenting on Dt XXV 9 וענתה ואמרה.

[26] Snh XI 2 commenting on Dt XVII 12 אשר יעשה בזדון.
Ker I 2 commenting on Num XV 29 לעשה בשגגה (Sages).

[27] Ḥag I 1 commenting on Ex XXIII 14 (Hillelites) רגלים.

[28] Snh VI 5 commenting on Dt XXI 23 (R Meir) כי קללת אלהים.

[29] Zeb VI 2 commenting on Lev VI 2 הוא העלה.

[30] The latter meaning given in B Ḳam IX 11 in commenting on Num V 8 is, as Se || Brs b B Ḳam 110a and SZ reveal, arrived at by a critical study of the text.

[31] Ḥull XII 3 commenting on Dt XXII 6.

[32] So R Jose the Galilean in Ḥull VIII 4 commenting on Dt XIV 21. Only the context decides him in favor of the former. Cf. also the etymology of this word in Meklenburg's הכתב והקבלה on Ex XXIII 19 where it is given a ground meaning similar to שֶׁגֶר Ex XIII 12.

[33] Soṭ VI 3 commenting on Dt XXIV 1 ערות דבר.

[34] Giṭṭ IX 10 Shammaiites and Hillelites on the same passage. The issue is clarified in Se || Br b Giṭṭ 99a and j. Cf. also Hor I 3 on דבר in Lev IV 13 for which Meklenburg (הכתב והקבלה Lev IV 13) cites as further proof Ex V 11 אין נגרע מעבודתכם דבר.

[35] The former meaning is the one given in B Meṣ IV 10 in a comment on Ex XXII 20 וגר לא תונה as the result of an exegesis given in Br b B Meṣ 58b. The possibility of either of the two significances is definitely mentioned in MS. Cf. also Malbim hereon.

[36] Soṭ VIII 2 commenting on Dt XX 4 ה' אלהיכם ההלך עמכם. The first interpretation gives to the expression the first meaning, the second the second meaning.

[37] The two constructions are cited in Snh VIII 4 commenting on Dt XXI 20 בננו זה. The Babylonian Talmud calls attention to these two different meanings attributed to the same word b Snh 71b האי מיבעי ליה זה ולא סומין.

[38] Ben Zoma Ber I 5 commenting on Dt XVI 3 כל ימי חייך states that without כל he would have interpreted ימי as days in contrast with the nights according to the principle mentioned above of תפשת מרובה. Cf. also Zab II 3 where יום Ex XXI 21 is identified as a complete diurnal cycle as indicated by the following יומים according to the exegesis given in M and MS q. v.

[39] Ḥull V 5 commenting on Lev XXII 28. Were it not for the analogy of Gen I 5, the diurnal cycle would have been reckoned beginning with the morning. (B Zoma Sa || Br b Ḥull 83a).

[40] Arakh IV 4 commenting on Lev XXVII 5 and 6. The meaning is determined by Lev XXVII 7 ואם מבן ששים שנה ומעלה. Cf. also Sa.

[41] Makk I 6 Sages commenting on Dt XIX 21. Dt XIX 19 כאשר זמם לעשות indicates the latter meaning according to the Sages. Malbim and Meklenburg, however, derive the thought from the use of the preposition ב instead of the usual תחת as in Ex XXI 23 ff.

[42] Bekh IX 1 commenting on Lev XXVII 32 בקר וצאן. The contrast with בקר proves that it means Kleinvieh in this instance.

[43] Men XI 5 Abba Saul commenting on Lev XXIV על המערכת decides in favor of the latter on the basis of ועליו מטה מנשה Num II 20. The entertainment of the two possibilities is more explicitly stated in Br b Men 98a in the name of Rabbi (אחה אומר על בסמוך או אינו אלא על ממש) who cites as support for this interpretation Ex XL 3 וסכת על הארן את הפרכת.

[44] Ed II 10 R Joḥanan b Nuri commenting on Is LXVI 23 ומדי שבת בשבתו. The first שבת refers to the feast of Shabuoth, the second to the seven week cycle between Passover and Shabuoth.

[45] Men XI 7 R Jose says that Ex XXV 30 תמיד implies even the case where in order to put on a fresh supply of bread the table of the shewbread was left for a moment without bread.

[46] Dt VI 7 מאדך in Ber IX 5. The word recurs as a substantive only in II Kings XXIII 25 in the same formula.

[47] Ez XLVI 22 in Midd II 5. It is a hapaxlegomenon.

[48] As in תעולל Dt XXIV 21 and Lev XIX 10 given in Peah VII 4.

[49] Snh VI 5 R Meir commenting on Dt XXI 23 קללת אלהים תלוי remarks: . . . שכינה מה הלשון אומרת קלני מראשי.

[50] Neg X 1 R Joḥanan b Nuri tries to determine by popular usage (מה הלשון אומרת) what is meant by דק Lev XIII 30.

[51] דמע in Ex XXII 28 מלאתך ודמעך לא תאחר, is interpreted as תרומה (Ter III 6). Cf. MS where this definition is explicitly given and Dobschütz p. 32, note 2.

[52] Cf. note 21. [53] Cf. note 29. [54] Cf. note 24.

[55] Dt XXII 17. [56] Snh X 6. [57] Ex XXIII 5.

[58] B Meṣ II 10. [59] Cf. note 27.

[60] Jer XXXIII 25 (יומם ולילה) בריתי "my covenant".

[61] Ned III 11. [62] Ex XXII 20 "stranger". [63] B Meṣ IV 10.

[64] I Sam XVII 36 (הפלשתי) הערל (הזה) "uncircumcised".
II Sam I 20 (בנות פלשתים . . . בנות) הערלים "uncircumcised".
Jer IX 25 (כי כל הגוים) ערלים "uncircumcised".

[65] Ned III 11. [66] Ex XXIII 2 "many". [67] Snh I 6.

[68] Pr IV 2 "my teaching" Gen XXVI 5 "my teachings".

[69] Ab III 14.

[70] Lev XXIV 22 "ordinance".

[71] Snh IV 1. [72] Is XXVIII 8 בלי מקום "without space".

[73] Ab III 3.

[74] Ps LXXXII 1 בקרב אלהים ישפט (Ab III 6).

[75] Is LVIII 8 כבוד ה' יאספך (Soṭ I 9).

[76] Is XLII 21 יגדיל תורה ויאדיר (Makk III 16).

[77] Is XXX 22 תזרם כמו דוה (Sabb IX 1 || Ab Zar III 6).

[78] Dt XXIV 7 והתעמר בו ומכרו (Snh XI 1 R Judah. MT quotes Dt XXII 14 in support of this interpretation).

[79] Lev XXI 12 ומן המקדש לא יצא (Snh II 1 R Meir). However b Snh 19a construes the interpretation of R Meir as מקדושתו לא יצא making of מקדש an abstract noun like מכתב, מצוה etc.

[80] Dt VII 26 שקץ תשקצנו (Ab Zar III 6 anon.).

[81] Lev I 3 לרצנו (Arakh V 6).

[82] Pr XI 27 ודרש רעה תבואנו (Peah VIII 9).

[83] Joel II 23 ויורד לכם גשם . . . בראשון (Taan I 2 R Meir).

NOTES III

[1] B Ḳam IV 4 commenting on Ex XXI 28. Cf. also MS || Br b B Ḳam 41a שור האיצטדין פטור לפי שאינו אלא מעושה.

[2] Dt VII 26.

[3] Cf. Ab Zar III 6 anon.

[4] Ḥag I 7 R Simon b Jochai commenting on Eccl I 15 מעות לא יוכל לתקן.

[5] Dt XVII 12.

[6] Snh XI 2. That the הפעיל is one of the possible constructions of this expression is evident from Mt || Br b Snh 88b מכאן אמרו אינו חייב עד שיורה לאחרים לעשות כהוראתו או שיעשה הוא כהוראתו. It is clinched by Br j אמר ר' הילא תני ר' ישמעאל כן אשר יעשה לא הוא שיעשה which definitely construes it as הפעיל not as קל. Cf. also Meklenburg הכתב והקבלה ad loc.

[7] Makhsh I 3 R Joshua in the name of Abba Jose Ḥali Kuphri of Tibeon interpreting the view of the Hillelites. The rendering is supported by O and PJ but not by Pš which translates נפלו. Cf. also Meklenburg הכתב והקבלה ad loc. that the הֻפְעַל bears in mind the agent whereas the נִפְעַל is used in cases where the agent is unimportant or absent. The emphasis being on the act as e. g. in ונכרתה הנפש Num IX 13.

[8] Lev XI 38. [9] Is XXV 8. [10] M Ḳaṭ III 9.

[11] Lev XI 33.

[12] Soṭ V 2. This is Malbim's construction of the difficult passage. Cf. the references given in II note 1.

[13] Snh X 1 commenting on Is LX 21.

[14] Lev V 2.

[15] Shebu II 5 R Eliezer. [16] ibid. R Aḳiba.

[17] Dt XXII 1 in B Meṣ II 9.

[18] Ex XXIII 5 in B Meṣ II 10.

[19] Dt XXII 7 in Ḥull XII 2.

[20] Cf. the references in notes 17, 18 and 19.

[21] Num XVIII 15.

[22] Bekh VIII 9. [23] Lev XIX 20.

[24] Ker II 5 (חציה שפחה וחציה בת חורין). This is how Malbim explains R Aḳiba's point of view. Cf. also PJ ומתפרקא כולה עד כ ד ו ן לא איתפריקת

[25] Dt VI 7.

[26] Ber I 3. According to b Ber 11a the Shammaiites may have regarded this construction as temporal as well as an indication of manner: בשעת שכיבה שכיבה ממש ובשעת קימה קימה ממש.

[27] So Snh I 6 commenting on Ex XXIII 2. This independent use of the infinitive construct, analogous to the Latin future passive participle impersonal, is reflected by O and PJ which translate שלים דינא and סטי דינא respectively.

[28] Lev V 4.

[29] Shebu III 5 R Ishmael. But R Aḳiba agrees with him for he derives the prohibition of oaths regarding the past from the summary לכל אשר יבטא. Cf. Sa.

[30] Ex XV 1 ויאמרו לאמר.

[31] Soṭ V 4 R Aḳiba. Cf. the analysis of the sources namely Tos Soṭ VI 2 and 3, Br b Soṭ 30b, j, M and MS in Elbogen's Studien zur Geschichte des jüdischen Gottesdienstes, Berlin 1907, p. 6 ff.

[32] Ibid. R Nehemiah. The Babylonian Talmud explains the controversy by saying: רבי עקיבא סבר לאמר אמילתא קמייתא i. e. "saying (always): אשירה לה' כי גאה גאה as in Ex XV 21, whereas R Nehemiah holds "ויאמרו" דאמור כולהו בהדי הדדי "לאמר" דפתח משה ברישא i. e. "They recited (responding) לאמר=to (Moses') prompting".

[33] Jer XVII 7.

[34] Peah VIII 9.

[35] Dt XXVI 14.

[36] Maas Sh V 12. Se explains more fully: בין שהוא טמא ואני טהור או שהוא טהור ואני טמא. Cf. also Malbim hereon.

[37] Dt XXII 2 in B Meṣ II 7.

[38] Ex XXII 5.

[39] B Ḳam VI 4 R Simon.

[40] Dt XXV 10.

[41] Yab XII 6. MT says explicitly: אין לי אלא זקנים הדיוטות מניין ת"ל ונקרא שמו בישראל i. e. by ordinary Israelites. But see PJ which would seem to point against this rendering.

[42] Cf. I notes 32 and 33.

[43] Gen. V 2.

[44] Cf.[44] Cf. Tos Yab VIII 4 || Br b Yab 62a with the authorities reversed: ר' נתן אומר ב"ש אומרים זכר ונקבה ב"ה אומרין או זכר או נקבה.

[45] Yab VI 6.

[46] Lev XXVII 10.

[47] Tem I 2 anon. Cf. Sa || Br b Tem 9a for a parallel controversy about the construction of בהמה which is construed by R Simon as a singular and his colleagues as a collective. The connection between this and the Mishnah is noted in b ibid.

[48] Dt XXII 6.

[49] Ḥull XII 2.

[50] Gen I 28.

[50a] Yab VI 6 anon. Cf. b Yab 65a and j.

[51] Num VI 12.

[52] Naz III 5 anon. Cf. also the reference under I note 52 D במקהלות and הזכרים.

[53] Gen I 10.

[54] Parah VIII 8 || Miḳw V 4.

[55] Gen IV 10.

[56] Snh IV 5. The other interpretation construes it as numerical דמו ודם זרעיותיו.

[57] Num V 22.

[58] Soṭ II 5 R Meir.

[59] Ibid. anon. Acc. to Se R Meir prescribed only two oaths אמן שלא נטמיתי אמן שלא אטמא which are included in SZ in a longer list which can only represent the view of his opponents. Hence it is to be inferred that the opponents of R Meir construed אמן אמן distributively.

[60] Tem I 2.

[61] Parah VIII 8 || Miḳw V 4.

[62] Dt XX 2.

[63] Soṭ VIII 1 זה כהן משוח מלחמה. MT || Br b Soṭ 42a says more explicitly: הכהן . . . יכול כל כהן שירצה ת"ל ודברו השוטרים מה שוטרים בממונה אף כהן בממונה. It is possible that the reading should be המיומן "the distinguished" as in b Hor 12a where the Amora Raba explains המשיח שאין משיח על גביו as המיומן שבמשיחים.

[64] Ps I 5.

[65] Snh X 3. T translates ביומא רבא.

[66] Lev XXII 14.

[67] Ter VI 6. Cf. this use of the article in Gen XVI 6 עשי לה הטוב בעיניך.

[68] Ibid.

[69] Cf. notes 64 and 65.

[70] Lev I 3.

[71] Arakh V 6. O and PJ translate לרעוא ליה and לרעוא עלוי, which as Malbim and Meklenburg remark would be proper for לרצון לו (Cf. Ex XXVIII 38 לרצון להם and Lev XXII 20 לרצון . . . להם) but not for לרצנו.

[72] Dt XIX 4. [73] Makk II 5.

[74] Num XXX 10.

[75] Ned XI 9. Br b Ned 89a quotes the opposing views of R Aḳiba and R Ishmael giving as justification for the view of the latter: עד שיהא נדר בשעת אלמנות, and of the former, whose view according to R Ḥisda corresponds to that of the Mishnah: הרי הוא אומר כל אשר אסרה על נפשה עד שיהא איסורי נדר בשעת אלמנות . . .

[76] Dt XXI 23.

[77] Snh VI 5 R Meir. The exegesis is clearer in MT.

[78] Dt XV 2. [79] Shebi X 8. [80] Dt XIX 4.

[81] Shebi X 8 || Makk II 8. [82] Cf. note 76.

[83] Snh VI 4. [84] ibid. [85] Ex XIII 2.

[86] Bekh VIII 1 Rabbi Jose the Galilean.

[87] Ex XIII 13. [88] Bekh I 1. [89] Cf. note 87.
[90] Cf. note 88. [91] Lev XXV 33. [92] Arakh IX 8 Rabbi
[93] Dt XXIV 17.
[94] B Meṣ IX 13. Se, Tos B Meṣ X 10, Br b B Meṣ 115a and Br j quote also another view that עשירה ממשכנין אותה.
[95] Cf. note 91. [96] Arakh IX 8 Sages. [97] Dt XXIV 1.
[98] Giṭṭ IX 10 Shammaiites. [99] Soṭ VI 3.
[100] Cf. note 97. This is the converse of the use of conjunctive ו to express the genitive relation as in Gen III 16 עצבונך והרנך.
[101] Giṭṭ IX 10 Hillelites according to Se || Br b Giṭṭ 90a.
[102] Ex XII 6. [103] Pes V 5. [104] Dt XXII 6.
[105] Ḥull XII 2. [106] Dt XIII 17. [107] Snh X 6.
[108] Dt XII 17.
[109] Zeb IX 5. This interpretation is more explicit in Se and Sa Lev I 9 || Br b Zeb 85b ff.
[110] Gen I 5. [111] Ḥull V 5. [112] Lev VI 2.
[113] Zeb IX 1 R Joshua כל הראוי לאשים אם עלה לא ירד.
[114] Ex XIII 2.
[115] Bekh VIII 1 R Jose the Galilean עד שיפטרו רחם בבני שראל.
[116] Lev XXIV 2.
[117] Men VIII 5 זך כתית למאור ולא זך כתית למנחות
[118] Lev XVI 30.
[119] Yoma VIII 9 R Elazar b Azariah עבירות שבין אדם למקום.
[120] Dt XII 2.
[121] Ab Zar III 5 R Jose the Galilean אלהיהם על ההרים ולא ההרים אלהיהם.
[122] Dt VII 25.
[123] Ab Zar III 5 הן מותרין ומה שעליהם אסורים.
[124] Gen XII 6. [125] Soṭ VII 5. [126] Cf. note 112.
[127] Zeb IX 1 Rabban Gamaliel כל הראוי למזבח אם עלה לא ירד.
[128] Dt XXIV 1. [129] Giṭṭ III 2. [130] Lev XXI 7.
[131] Yab X 3. [132] Lev IV 28. [133] Ker VI 7.
[134] Dt XXII 2. [135] B Meṣ II 7. [136] Lev IV 23.
[137] Ker IV 3. Cf. Sa. [138] Dt XVII 16.
[139] Snh II 4. Cf. also Malbim and Meklenburg ad loc.
[140] Dt XVII 17. [141] Snh II 4. [142] Dt XIII 17.
[143] Snh X 6. [144] Ex XXIII 19. [145] Bik I 2.
[146] Ex XIII 7. [147] Pes II 2. [148] Lev VII 34.
[149] Ḥull X 1. [150] Dt XXV 5. [151] Yab III 9. Cf. Malbim.
[152] Dt XXIII 19. [153] Tem VI 3. [154] Ex XLI 23.
[155] Midd IV 1. [156] Dt XXI 20. [157] Snh VIII 5.
[158] Dt XXIX 27. [159] Snh X 3 R Aḳiba. [160] Cf. note 154.
[161] Snh VIII 4. Cf. Gesenius' Grammar ¶136d for this use of the particle.
[162] Cf. note 156. [163] Snh X 3 R Eliezer. Cf. also note 161.
[164] Lev VI 16. [165] Sheḳ I 4. [166] II note 45.
[167] Dt XIII 17.

[168] Snh X 6 R Jose the Galilean: לא תבנה אפילו גנות ופרדסים. The reading of MT proves that the controversy is over the interpretation of עוד. Cf. also Malbim.

[169] ibid. R Aḳiba: לכמו שהיתה אינה נבנית אבל נעשית היא גנות ופרדסים.

[170] Cf. II note 43.

[171] Lev XXIII 14.

[172] Men X 5 R Judah והלא מן התורה הוא אסור.

[173] Cf. II note 40 and b Men 68b which assumes that Rabban Joḥanan b Zakkai holds עד ולא עד בכלל.

[174] Cf. II note 57. [175] Num XI 16.

[176] Snh I 6 anon. ומשה על גביהן. b Snh 16b explains the exegesis of the anon. author correctly: עמך ואת בהדייהו.

[177] ibid. R Judah by inference. [178] Lev IX 22.

[179] Soṭ VII 6 || Tam VII 2 R Judah. Cf. Gesenius' Handwörterbuch אל Anmerkung.

[180] Dt XXV 2. [181] Makk III 10 anon. Cf. also Se and Malbim.

[182] Note 40. [183] Lev XIV 35. [184] Neg XII 5.

[185] Ex XIII 7.

[186] Pes II 2. MS states more explicitly רואה אתה לאחרים. Cf. also the discussion in Meklenburg's הכתב והקבלה ad locum on this use of ל with the pronominal suffixes.

[187] Lev XXVII 22. [188] Arakh VII 5 R Judah and R Simon.

[189] Dt XXXI 10. [190] Soṭ VII 8. [191] Is XLI 4.

[192] Ed II 9. [193] Dt XXIX 27. [194] Snh X 3.

[195] Cf. S, V and Pš. [196] Joel II 23. [197] Taan I 2 R Meir.

[198] Cf. S, V and Pš. [199] Is XXIX 1. [200] Midd IV 7.

[201] Ex XXIII 19 and Dt XXIII 19. [202] Bik I 9.

[203] Parah II 3. [204] Ex XXIII 16.

[205] Bik I 3. Such a construction would make בכורי מעשיך || למועד and בצאת השנה. To construe it as a genitive with the already determined הקציר would be contrary to the grammar of the Hebrew language.

[206] Gen V 2. [207] Yab VI 6 Hillelites.

[208] Dt XXI 2.

[209] Soṭ IX 1 R Judah. b Soṭ 44b ff says of R Judah's opponent ווי לא משמע ליה.

[210] Num V 29. [211] Soṭ V 1. [212] Gen V 2.

[213] Yab VI 6 Shammaiites. Cf. also note 44 for full references bearing out this interpretation of the view of the Shammaiites.

[214] Dt XXI 2.

[215] I quote Br b Soṭ 44b which is the basis of the remark in the Mishnah Soṭ IX 1.

[216] So j which interprets the view of anon. correctly by saying he explains זקניך שהן שפטיך. Cf. also b Soṭ 44b למיוחדין שבשופטיך and ו"ו (למנינא) לא משמע ליה. See Malbim and Meklenburg ad loc.

[217] Ex XXXIV 21. [218] Shebi I 4 R Ishmael.

[219] Num XXX 14. [220] Ned X 7 Sages. [221] Lev XXVII 10.

[222] Tem I 1 R Aḳiba. [223] Tem I 2 R Simon. [224] Dt XVI 2.

[225] Men VII 6. [226] Dt XVII 17.

[227] Snh II 4 R Simon. Cf. b Snh 21a למימרא דר' ... שמעון לא דריש טעמא דקרא.

[228] Lev V 2. [229] Shebu II 5 R Eliezer.

[230] Lev XIV 36.

[231] Neg XII 5 R Judah as appears from the remarks of his opponent R Simon q. v. Cf. also Malbim.

[232] Cf. note 230. [233] Neg XII 5. [234] Dt XXII 2.

[235] B Meṣ II 7. [236] Dt XVII 17.

[237] Snh II 4 R Judah. Cf. b Snh 21a למימרא דר' יהודה דריש טעמא דקרא.

[238] II Chr XXXIII 13. [239] Snh X 2 anon. [240] Lev V 2.

[241] Shebu II 5 R Aḳiba. [242] Dt XXII 29. [243] Ket III 5.

[244] Is LVIII 8. [245] Soṭ I 9. [246] Dt XXV 3.

[247] Makk III 15. [248] Dt XXIV 21.

[249] Peah VII 7 R Aḳiba. Cf. also Sa.

[250] Cf. note 248.

[251] Peah VII 7 R Eliezer. According to j it would seem that R Eliezer also regards כי as temporal.

[252] Dt XXIV 1. [253] Giṭṭ IX 10 Shammaiites.

[254] ibid. Hillelites. [255] cf. note 252.

[256] ibid. R Aḳiba. Cf. also the remark of b Giṭṭ 90a that the controversy between the Shammaiites and Hillelites vs R Aḳiba rages about the construction of כי the former interpreting it causally כי=דהא, the latter alternatively כי=אי נמי. Cf. Meklenburg ad loc.

[257] Ex XXII 7. [258] B Meṣ III 12. [259] Dt XIX 5.

[260] Makk II 2. [261] Ex XXI 21.

[262] Zab II 3. Cf. Meklenburg, הכתב והקבלה ad loc. He cites as proof Ex XXI 6 והגישו אל הדלת או אל המזוזה i. e. "namely" = "or rather".

[263] Dt XVI 17.

[264] Ḥag I 5. [265] Ps CXIX 126.

[266] Ber IX 5. Cf. also the remark of the Amora Raba in b Ber 63a who construes the subordinate clauses as causal.

NOTES IV

[1] Makk III 10 anon. S and V have the same division.

[2] Men VIII 7.

[3] Soṭ VII 5. Br j gives view of R Simon based on the massoretic punctuation.

[4] Snh I 6. [5] Makk III 15.

[6] Arakh VIII 6 Sages. According to them קדש קדשים is in apposition to חרם for הוא חל על קדשי קדשים ועל קדשים קלים.

[7] Arakh VIII 6 Sages. [8] Soṭ VII 4 R Judah.

[9] Men VIII 7.

[10] Men IX 3 R Eliezer b Jacob. Cf. also Br b Men 89a.

[11] Neg XIV 10 R Aḳiba.
[12] Men IX 3 anon.
[13] Neg XIV 10 R Joḥanan b Nuri.
[14] Midd III 1.
[15] Chapter I.
[16] Pes IX 2.
[17] Ned III 11.
[18] Gen XVII 1.
[19] Ned III 11.
[20] Yad IV 7.
[21] Soṭ III 2.

[22] This was noted by b Soṭ 19b: במאי קמיפלגי . . . תלתא קראי כתיבי. Cf. also Se which is quoted there and SZ and Malbim.

[23] Chapter I.
[24] Makk II 6.
[25] Makk I 6.
[26] Zeb XIV 1.
[27] Meg III 3.
[28] Ab III 2.
[29] Makk III 15.
[30] Jud XVI 21 (Soṭ I 8).
[31] Soṭ I 8.
[32] II Sam XVIII 15 (Soṭ I 8).
[33] II Sam XV 6 (Soṭ I 8).
[34] II Sam XVIII 14 (Soṭ I 8).
[35] Ex II 4 (Soṭ I 9).
[36] Num XII 15 (Soṭ I 9).
[37] Gen L 7 (Soṭ I 9).
[38] Ex XIII 19 (Soṭ I 9).
[39] Dt XXXIV 6 (Soṭ I 9).
[40] Sabb VIII 7.
[41] Sabb IX 3.

[42] ibid. and Sabb XIX 3. Sic also V: die tertio quando gravissimus vulnerum dolor est.

[43] Sabb IX 4.
[44] Taan I 7.
[45] Taan III 3.
[46] Snh VI 1.
[47] Soṭ VIII 1.
[48] R Hash III 8.
[49] ibid.
[50] Soṭ IX 6.
[51] Taan IV 8.
[52] Yab IX 6.
[53] Yab XII 6.
[54] Soṭ II 2.
[55] Soṭ VII 5.
[56] Soṭ VIII 4.
[57] B Meṣ VIII 1
[58] Snh II 4.
[59] Snh VI 4.
[60] Midd III 8.
[61] Midd IV 1.
[62] Peah VIII 9.
[63] Sabb IX 3 and Yoma VI 8.
[64] Cf. Tossafoth Yomtob ad loc.
[65] Yad IV 4.
[66] לעתיד לבא M Ḳaṭ III 9.
[67] Midd II 5.
[68] Peah V 6 and VII 3.
[69] Taan III 8.
[70] Sukk II 6 and Ḥag I 6.
[71] Ḳidd I 10.
[72] Snh X 3.
[73] ibid.
[74] Snh III 7.

[75] Ab V 18. Cf. also Tos Soṭ IV 9, Se and MT where this interpretation is more explicit.

[76] Snh I 6. Evidently מלינים is here construed as a causative הפעיל like וילונו in verse 36.

[77] Snh X 3.
[78] ibid.
[79] ibid.
[80] Hor III 3.
[81] Snh I 6.

[82] Soṭ IX 6. Tos Soṭ IX 3 remarks hereon: שלשה דברים זה בצד זה מה שאמר זה לא אמר זה and cites other instances similar to this. Cf. also j.

[83] Yab XII 6 anon.
[84] Maas Sh V 13.
[85] Ab III 14.
[86] Pes X 5.
[87] Ab III 6.
[88] Neg XII 6.
[89] Soṭ IX 11.
[90] Soṭ IX 12.
[91] Ab V 19.
[92] Uḳṣ III 12.

NOTES V

[1] Cf. II note 13. [2] Cf. ibid. [3] Cf. II note 9.

[4] Cf. ibid. [5] Cf. ibid. [6] Cf. II note 7.

[7] Cf. II notes 12 and 18. [8] Cf. II note 17.

[9] Cf. II notes 5 and 11. [10] Snh X 3 anon.

[11] R Hash III 2 R Jose. [12] Ned III 11. [13] Miḳw IX 2.

[14] Snh X 6 R Jose the Galilean. Tos Snh XIV 6 quotes the entire verse and cites a different explanation of והיתה תל עולם by R Aḳiba, the opponent of R Jose the Galilean, indicating that the latter considered the two parts equivalent.

[15] Sabb IX 1 || Ab Zar III 6 R Aḳiba. The indication of separation is clearer in צא than in the difficult תזרם.

[16] Bik I 3. Cf. also III note 205 for the construction.

[17] Yad IV 3 סוד = "secret "not" counsel".

[18] Parah VIII 8 || Miḳw V 4 R Judah. ימים is probably construed as a plural of extension, i. e. a logical singular, so as to be parallel with ארץ, or perhaps because מקוה is singular.

[19] Ber I 3 Hillelites according to the explanation quoted in Yalḳuṭ וב"ה ובלכתך בדרך למה לי שמע מינה דאפילו בדרך נמי קרי. Since ובלכתך בדרך is temporal ובשכבך ובקומך must also be. Cf. also Se: ובשכבך יכול אפילו בחצי היום ת"ל בשבתך בביתך ובלכתך בדרך דרך ארץ דברה תורה כלשון בני אדם.

[20] Soṭ VII 5. [21] Ḥull V 5.

[22] Ned III 11. [23] Zeb IX 5.

[24] Ḥull XII 2 אפרחים או ביצים are descriptions of the קן צפור and, therefore, generic plurals so as to be parallel to צפור. Cf. also III note 48.

[25] Ned III 11. [26] Cf. note 18.

[27] Naz IX 5 R Nehorai. [28] B Meṣ IX 13. [29] Peah IV 10.

[30] Peah VII 3. [31] Bekh IX 1.

[32] B Ḳam VI 4. The equation of שדה = עפר is more clearly stated in M and MS. Cf. also Malbim and b B Ḳam 60a: שדה ל"ל לאתויי לחכה נירו וסכסכה אבניו ולכתוב רחמנא שדה ולא בעי הנך צריכא דאי כתב רחמנא שדה הוה אמינא מה שבשדה אין מידי אחרינא לא קמ"ל.

[33] B Ḳam IX 11. Cf. II note 30 for references to the full exegesis.

[34] Men XI 5 Abba Saul. [35] Maas Sh V 12. Cf. Malbim.

[36] M Ḳaṭ III 9. [37] Cf. III notes 217–223.

[38] Cf. I note 41. [39] Ab Zar II 5.

[40] This follows the version of Rashi as against that of Geiger in his Urschrift p. 401 ff. Rashi's quotation is more acceptable because, assuming an unvocalized text, there could be no indication as to gender from שמניך whereas על כן עלמות אהבוך clearly indentifies the addressee as a male. This does not invalidate the theory of Geiger that the controversey was as to to whether the reading should be דֹּדֶיךָ or דַּדַּיִךְ. It only reverses the authorities.

Our reading is confirmed by that of Tos Parah IX 3 which ascribes to R Ishmael the reading דדיך and to R Joshua that of דודיך. Furthermore in b

Ab Zar 35a דודיך is assumed as the correct (therefore final) reading because Israel, the bride, is said to be addressing God, the bridegroom, in these words.

[41] Ḥull VIII 4 R Jose the Galilean.

[42] Yab VI 6 R Joḥanan b Baroḳa.

[43] Arakh IV 4.

[44] Arakh IX 8 Rabbi. Cf. Sa.

[45] Ab III 2.

[46] Yab VIII 2.

[47] Snh I 6.

[48] Ab Zar I 9.

[49] I notes 8 and 9.

[50] The expression is actually used in Se and MT || Br b Soṭ 33b and Br j Soṭ VII 5 the source of the analogy of אלוני מרה (Dt XI 30) = אלון מורה Gen XII 6. Cf. also Bacher I p. 13 ff.

[51] Soṭ VI 3.

[52] Soṭ VII 3.

[53] Soṭ VII 4.

[54] Soṭ VII 5.

[55] Snh I 6 and Hor I 4.

[56] Men XI 5 Abba Saul.

[57] Ḥull V 5.

[58] Naz IX 5 R Nehorai.

[59] Snh VIII 2.

[60] Ḥull XI 2 Shammaiites.

[61] ibid. Hillelites.

[62] Yad IV 4 R Joshua.

[63] I. e. except עדה Snh I 6, זולל וסבא, צאן. In the case of על the formula is והלא כבר נאמר.

[64] Snh X 3 R Eliezer.

[65] Tos Snh XIII 9 R Judah b Bathyra vs R Aḳiba.

[66] Soṭ IX 5.

[67] MT, b Soṭ 46b and j. Sic also S and V.

[68] b ibid.

[69] MT.

[70] Snh XI 1.

[71] MT.

[72] Tem I 2.

[73] Sa.

[74] Soṭ VIII 4.

[75] MT.

[76] Soṭ V 5.

[77] Br b Soṭ 31a R Meir.

[78] Pes IX 2.

[79] Se R Eliezer and R Judah || Tos Pes VIII 2 || Br b Pes 94b. Cf. also j.

[80] Tem VI 2.

[81] Tos Tem IV 6.

[82] Tem VI 2.

[83] Tos Tem IV 4.

[84] Yab VIII 2.

[85] b Yab 76b. Cf. also Malbim.

[86] Soṭ VIII 1.

[87] b Soṭ 42a and j.

[88] Ket III 5.

[89] j ר׳ ירמיה ר׳ חייה בשם רשב״ל לא יאמר ולו תהיה לאשה זה המוציא שם רע שאינו צריך שכבר היא תחת ידו ומה ת״ל ולו תהיה לאשה תלמד הימינה לגזירה שוה מתדרש ולו תהיה ולו תהיה מה לו תהיה שנ׳ להלן אשה הראויה לו אף לו תהיה שנ׳ כאן אשה הראויה לו.

[90] Sabb IX 1 || Ab Zar III 6 R Aḳiba.

[91] Taan I 2 R Meir.

[92] Ned III 11.

[93] Ab III 6.

[94] Ab III 14.

[95] Yoma V 5.

[96] Soṭ VII 8.

[97] Ibid.

[98] Dt XIII 17.

[99] Snh X 3.

[100] Ibid. R Eliezer.

[101] Cf. I note 7.

[102] Sheḳ VI 7. Cf. Malbim.

[103] Soṭ V 3.

[104] Snh I 6.

[105] Ed II 9.

[106] Zeb IX 5. Cf. also I note 7.

[107] Arakh VIII 6. Cf. also Sa.

[108] Arakh VIII 7.

[109] Peah VII 7.

[110] Men VII 6.

[111] Makk I 6.

[112] Zab II 3. The full interpretation is found in M and MS.

[113] Makk III 10 anon. According to Malbim there is a contradiction between כדי רשעתו במספר and ארבעים יכנו Hence במספר is read with ארבעים,

which is taken to stand in opposition with it, and it is construed as "up to the number".

[114] Yab XII 6. Cf. Malbim.

[115] B Meṣ III 12 Hillelites. Cf. M || j and Br b B Meṣ 44a.

[116] Snh XI 1 R Judah. Cf. M Ex XXI 17.

[117] Zeb XIII. Cf. Sa and Malbim.

[118] Pes IX 2 R Jose according to Malbim as borne out by Tos Pes VIII 3 R Jose the Galilean. Cf. Br b Pes 94a and b and also j.

[119] Soṭ III 2 R Simon. Cf. Se SZ and b Soṭ 19b: במאי קמיפלגי תלתא קראי כתיבי . . . ור"ש סבר ואחר ישקה לגופו שמקריב את מנחתה ואחר כך משקה. Cf. also j.

[120] Naz IX 5 R Nehorai. [121] Snh X 3 R Eliezer.

[122] Ber I 5.

[123] Cf. M, Tos Ber I 12, Br b Ber 12b and j.

[124] Soṭ V 5. [125] Cf. b Soṭ 31a.

[126] Cf. I note 34 to 38 and III notes 128 to 153.

[127] Arakh VII 5 R Judah and R Simon. Cf. Sa || Br b Arakh 26b.

[128] Snh XI 4 R Judah. Cf. MT || Br b Snh 89a.

[129] Neg XII 6. Cf. Malbim.

[130] Makk III 10 anon. Cf. b Makk 22b.

[131] B Meṣ II 10. [132] Snh XI 2. [133] Cf. also Malbim.

[134] Ker I 2. [135] Tem I 2 R Simon. Cf. Malbim.

[136] The versions translate as if the original were יהיו.

[137] Sabb IX 2. Cf. j which bases the exegesis on the number of letters rather than the number of words.

[138] The form is unique. [139] Soṭ VI 3.

[140] Se || Br b Soṭ 31b. [141] Ḥull VIII 4.

[142] Cf. b Ḥull 113a and b. [143] Makk III 15. [144] Se.

[145] Cf. j on Soṭ VII 5 the opposing view בעשרים וארבע מקומות נקראו הכהנים לויים.

[146] Soṭ VII 5. [147] Snh I 6. [148] Soṭ IX 6.

;[149] Ab V 18. [150] Snh X 3. [151] Snh II 3 anon.

[152] Cf. Br b Snh 20a.

[153] Soṭ VIII 1 both interpretations. [154] Cf. j.

[155] Ḳidd III 4. Cf. also b Ḳidd 61a and b.

[156] Ab Zar III 3. Cf. Tos III 19 and Brs in b Ab Zar 43b, and j.

[157] Sabb VI 4. Cf. Br b Sabb 63a, and j.

NOTES VI

[1] Cf. I notes 7 ff. [2] Cf. the previous chapter

[3] Cf. chapter III.

[4] Cf. Gesenius' Hebrew Grammar, Oxford, 1909, p. 99 ff.

[5] Ibid. p. 100. [6] Cf. chapter II.

[7] שעטנז Cf. Mandelkern's Concordance.

[8] Wilhelm Gesenius' Hebräisches und aramäisches Handwörterbuch über das alte Testament, Leipzig, 1921.

[9] Dt VI 5. [10] Ber IX 5.

[11] Cf. Gesenius' Handwörterbuch. [12] Lev XIII 18.

[13] Neg IX 1. [14] Cf. Gesenius' Handwörterbuch.

[15] Lev XXI 18. [16] Bekh VII 3.

[17] Cf. Wahrmund, Handwörterbuch der neu-arabischen und deutschen Sprache, Giessen 1898.

[18] Ex XXII 28. [19] Ter III 6. [20] Dt XIX 3.

[21] Makk II 5. [22] Is LXVI 23. [23] Ed II 10.

[24] Ex XXIII 5. [25] B Meṣ II 10. [26] Cf. V note 131.

[27] Dt XIX 21. [28] Makk I 6 Pharisees.

[29] Cf. Malbim. [30] Ex XIII 7.

[31] Pes II 2. Cf. note on III (186).

[32] Ex XXIII 14. [33] Ḥag I 1.

[34] So Ex XXIII 17, Ex XXXIV 23.24.

[35] Is LXI 11. [36] Sabb IX 2. [37] I note 26 ff.

[38] I note 34 ff. [39] IV note 40 ff. [40] I note 21 ff.

[41] IV note 30 ff. [42] IV note 68–74.

[43] E. g. פָּנִים Cf. II note 2. [44] I note 21.

[45] Ibid. note 23. [46] Ibid. note 22.

[47] IV note 65 ff. and 75 ff.

[48] IV notes 62 and 63. [49] Soṭ IX 9.

[50] Soṭ IX 6. Cf. also the remarks about Ex XVII 11 and Num XXI 8 in R Hash III 8.

NOTES VII

(Note: Notes 52 and 56 of chapter I should be consulted for the respective passages.) Roman numerals in this section refer to the chapters of this book. The figures in parentheses refer to the numbers of the notes in the respective chapters.

1. V (21) and note.
2. Sic O, PJ, S, V and Pš.
3. III (54), V (18).
4. I (26) note and V (42).
5. III (50a). The remarks of b Yab 65a and j regarding the orthography of וכבשה clearly indicate that פרו ורבו were conceived as generic plurals.
6. III (56) and note. Sic also O.
7. III (56) and note. Sic also PJ.
8. III (44) note, III (213) and note.
9. III (207) and note.
10. [a] I. e. the spirit of life acc. to Br b Snh 108a: ר' יהודה בן בתירא אומר לא חיין ולא נדונין שנ' לא ידון רוחי. . . לא דין ולא רוח. [b] IV (77) and note. [c] II (16) note and (9) note, V (4). [d] Cf. Tos Snh XIII 6: איני דן בשעה שאני משלם שכר לצדיקים.
11. III (124)+(125) and notes. V (20) and note.

12. II (68)+(69) and notes. Cf. also V (94).
13. IV (42) and note. Sic S. Cf. also PJ.
14. IV (42) and note and cf. j which states: טעמא דר' אלעזר בן עזריה ויהי ביום השלישי בהיותם כאבים בהיותו כואב אין כתיב אלא בהיותם כאבים בשעה שכל איבריהם כואבים עליהם.
15. I (37) note. III (102)+(103) and notes.
17. [a] III (115). [b] III (86).
18. III (146)+(147) and notes. III (185)+(186) and notes. VI (30).
19. I (26) note.
20. Sic clearly V: "quiquid habueris masculini sexus", and also Pš דכרא.
21. III (87)+(88) and notes.
22. III (31) note. Sic S.
23. III (32) note.
24. [a] II (38) note. Cf. PJ and Malbim. [b] Cf. Meklenburg for this use of the conjunction או.
25. Sic also O and PJ which translate מותא i. e. "death", not merely "accident".
26. III (1) and note.
28. Cf. Malbim. Sic V.
29. Cf. Malbim. Sic S.
30. Cf. Tos B Ḳam V 7, M and Malbim. b B Ḳam 45b explains that the determination of the meaning is based on general experience.
31. Cf. previous note.
32. I (36) note, the definite article is used in the generic sense here. Cf. III (66), (67).
33. V (32) and note.
34. Sic S, V and Pš.
35. III (39).
36. [a] II (62) and (63) and notes. [b] II (35) and note. Sic also PJ and V (contristabis).
37. [a] II (20), VI (18)+(19) and notes. [b] II (51) and note. Sic also S, Pš, O and PJ. V gives this interpretation to דמעך. [c] II (51) and note. V gives this interpretation to מלאתך. Cf. Meklenburg ad loc.
38. [a] II (66)+(67) and notes. [b] The injunction is addressed to judges V (47). [c] IV (4) and note. [d] III (27) and note.
39. I (35) and III (18)+(20) and notes.
40. II (57) and (58), III (174), VI (24)+(25)+(26), V (132). Sic also O, PJ, S, V, and Pš.
41. Sic O, PJ, S, V, and Pš.
42. II (27) Cf. also VI (33)+(34).
43. III (204) and note, (205) and note, V (16).
44. III (144) +(145) and notes.
45. III (202) and note.
46. II (2) note.
47. II (45) and III (166).

48. II (45) and III (166).
49. Cf. I (32) III (42).
50. Cf. b Yoma 51b and III (44) and (155).
51. II (23).
52. III (89), (90) and notes.
54. III (217) and (218).
55. Cf. also MS R Judah and R Simon.
56. II (81) and note, III (70) and (71) and notes.
57. Cf. for this meaning of כל, i. e. when followed by the definite article, Gesenius' Handwörterbuch.
58. Meklenburg makes עדה ⇌ ועד both coming from the same root. That there was a difference between this "council of the judges" and the whole community of Israel he proves from Num XXVII 21 וכל בני ישראל אתו וכל העדה.
60. [a] III (136)+(137) and notes.
61. [a] Cf. Sa.
62. III (132)+(133) and notes.
63. III (229).
64. III (241). Sic also V.
65. III (28), (29) and notes.
66. V (102) and note.
67. II (53) and note.
68. III (113).
69. III (127).
70. I (36) note.
71. Cf. Malbim.
72. Cf. III (165).
73. III (165).
74. III (148)+(149) and note.
75. III (178)+(179) and notes.
76. II (1) note, III (12).
77. Sic O and PJ and especially S, V, and Pš.
78. III (7)+(8) and notes.
79. However cf. Malbim.
80. VI (12), (13), (14) and notes.
83. II (50) and note. Sic V.
84. II (50) and note. Sic S.
86. IV (12). Sic also S and V.
87. IV (10).
88. IV (11).
89. IV (13).
90. III (184) and note.
91. III (213). Sic O and S.
92. III (233). Sic also PJ, V and Pš.
93. I (32) note IV (88) and note.

95. Sic also O and PJ.
96. III (118)+(119) and notes.
97. V (29) and note. Sic also S.
99. V (30) and note. Sic also O, PJ and Pš: נתרא.
100. [a] Sic O, PJ, S and Pš. V has "opus". [b] The Mishnah plays on the ground meaning of the root from which שכיר is derived.
101. [a] II (9) note.
102. III (24) and note.
103. Sa quoting ר׳ ישמעאל states: דברה תורה כלשון בני אדם.
104. Same construction as in verses 30 and 37 where Massorah reveals the same accents.
105. This is the provisional construction in b Makk 21a.
106. Cf. Malbim hereon.
107. Sic S and V. Cf. Malbim.
108. III (130)+(131) and note. איש="husband," in contrast to בעל which may stand for "paramour". Cf. Hosea II 18.
109. II (79). However acc. to b Snh 19a R Meir interprets: ומקדושתו לא יצא.
110. This is literal.
111. VI (15)+(16)+(17) and notes.
112. Sic S, V and Pš. Meklenburg (הכתב והקבלה ad loc.) suggests that the author of this interpretation derived מרוח from רֶוַח "space" i. e. "hollow".
113. Sic O.
114. II (12) note. Sic also PJ.
115. II (18) note.
116. Sic O.
117. Sic PJ.
118. II (9) note. Sic S, V and Pš.
119. III (68).
120. III (67).
121. II (39) note, V (57) and note.
122. O and PJ תערעון=cause to occur.
123. I (36) note, II (1) note.
124. III (173) and note.
125. III (172).
126. Cf. Malbim. O and PJ intercalate: ואלפינון. V says "locutusque est Moyses super solemnitatibus."
127. III (116) and (117) and notes.
128. II (9) note.
129. II (43) and note and III (170). Sic also S and V.
130. II (43) and note, III (170) and V (56).
131. [a] This is a continuation of the preceding verse. Cf. Malbim. [b] II (71) and note.
132. I (26) note.
133. I (35) and note.

134. I (35) and note.
138. III (92) and V (44) and note.
139. III (96).
140. Cf. III (128) ff.
141. Sic also V.
142. II (40) and note, V (43).
143. V (72) and (73) and notes. Sic also PJ.
144. I (32) note.
145. III (222) and note.
146. III (47) and note.
147. III (47), V (136) and note.
148. IV (7) and note.
149. Cf. Sa || Br b 26b. Sic O, PJ, S, V, and Pš.
150. III (187) and note, V (127) and note.
151. IV (6). Sic O, PJ, S, V and Pš.
152. IV (6). The Mishnah states: שהוא חל על קדשי קדשים ועל קדשים קלים, i. e. קדש קדשים is conceived as being either in apposition to or in the genitive relation with חרם.
153. II (42) and note, V (31) and note.
154. II (43) and note, III (170) note, V (34).
155. [a] II (30) and note, V (33) and note. Sic also O and PJ. [b] Sic definitely PJ, S, V, and Pš.
156. V (139), (140) and note. Cf. also Gersonides (פירוש רלב"ג) ad loc. Sic also V: "testibus".
157. III (59) and note.
158. III (58) and (59) note.
159. Sic PJ מגילתא. Cf. Malbim.
160. IV (21), (22) and note, V (119) and note. Cf. b Soṭ 19b: לאחר כל המעשים כולן האמורין למעלה. Cf. also Malbim.
161. IV (21), (22) and note, V (119) and note. Cf. Malbim.
162. III (211).
163. Inferred from the fact that he does not accept R Akiba's interpretation
164. III (52) and note.
165. I (26) note.
166. Cf. clearer statement of the controversy in Tos Parah I 1 and also Malbim. The form is conceived as similar to that of Mishnaic רְבָעִי = "four-year old".
167. Sic clearly S. Cf. also Tos Parah I 1.
169. IV (16) and note, V (118) and note. Sic also PJ.
170. III (177).
171. III (176).
172. [a] IV (76) and note, V (147) and note.
173. I (38) note.
174. I (39) note and V (121).
175. V (134) and note.

176. I (38) note.
177. V (64) and (65).
178. I (35) note, III (21), (22) and notes.
179. IV (2) and note.
180. IV (9) and note.
181. III (74)+(75) and notes.
182. III (220). Cf. also b Ned 76b: בעלמא דרשי ק"ו ושאני הכא דאמר קרא אישה יקימנו ואישה יפירנו referring no doubt to the force of the repetition of אישה
183. Sic V.
184. I (38) note.
185. [a] V (55). Cf. also Malbim. [b] Cf. I Sam III 13, Ps LI 6.
186. [a] II (21).
187. II (46), VI (9)+(10)+(11) and notes. So also O, PJ and Pš.
188. II (9) note.
189. II (9) note.
190. Sic S and V which may be based on the remark of the Mishnah במאד מאד "very, very much".
191. Cf. Se and MT.
192. III (25) and (26). So also S and V.
193. III (25) and (26). Cf. also V (19) and note. So also Se, MT, PJ and Pš.
194. III (122), (123) and notes.
195. V (48).
196. II (80) and III (2) and (3) and note.
197. I. e. it is the proper name of a place, not common as the translations would have it.
198. III (120)+(121) and notes.
199. III (108)+(109) and notes, V (23) and note, V (106) and note.
200. II (13) note V (2). Cf. etymology given in Gesenius' Handwörterbuch.
201. III (106)+(107) and notes.
202. According to b Snh 45b there is no disagreement between R Aḳiba and R Ishmael about the above rendering דר"ע בעינן קרא כדכתיב.
203. III (142)+(143) and notes.
204. II (56) and note, (57) and note, V (98).
205. III (168) and note, V (14) and note.
206. III (169).
207. V (156) and note.
208. V (156) and note.
209. II (32) and note, V (142). Cf. the remark of b 113a that the fact that in Gen XXXVIII 20 גדי is determined by העזים indicates that without such a limitation it could be applied to the young of any domesticated mammal: הא כל מקום שנ' גדי סתם אפילו פרה ורחל במשמע.
210. II (32) and note and V (41).

211. II (21), (52) and note, III (79). A less ambiguous expression for "law" would be תורה, as in Num V 29, or חקה as in Num XIX 2.
212. III (224), (225) and notes, V (110) and note. However cf. Malbim on Se, and M on Ex XII 5, also O and PJ.
213. II (38) and note, and V (122)+(123) and note. Cf. also Malbim.
214. Cf. references in note on V (123). The main thought is believed to be contained in חייך with which ימי is merged. Prof. Ginzberg suggests that the life of the nation rather than that of the individual is referred to according to this view.
215. III (263) and note.
216. II (24)+(52) Meklenburg (הכתב והקבלה ad loc.) derives the idea of warning from עדים and cites as proof Gen XLIII 3 . . . העד העיד בנו האיש i. e. שנים עדים="two warners".
217. II (24)+(54).
218. III (6) and note, V (132) and note, (133) and note.
219. Cf. Tos Snh XI 7, b Snh 89a and MT.
220. Cf. previous note and V (128).
221. The emphasis is, as Malbim points out, due to the repetition of the phrase in the verse. Cf. also I (36) note.
222. III (138)+(139) and note.
223. Sic PJ.
224. III (237) and note. Sic PJ, S, V and Pš.
225. III (227) and note. Sic also O.
226. III (140)+(141) and notes. Cf. also Malbim.
227. [a] Sic also S. [b] Sic also PJ.
228. II (22). Cf. Se: ויהיו מכוונות כשתי שורות שבכרם. Sic also PJ תכונון לכון אורחא. VI (21), (22).
229. II (21) and note III (72)+(73) and notes.
230. II (21)+(52) and note, III (81). A less ambiguous expression for law would be תורה, as in Num V 29, or חקה as in Num XIX 2.
231. III (260).
232. II (41) and note.
233. II (41) and note.
234. III (62), (63) and notes.
235. V (87) and note.
236. IV (47), V (153) and (154). Cf. also II (36).
237. IV (47), V (153) and (154). Cf. also II (36).
238. Cf. Tos Soṭ VII 18 which quotes ר' אליעזר, and Se which quotes ר' אליעזר בן יעקב as saying: אין לי במשמע אלא כרם. Cf. Malbim on Se. The Br as quoted in j says distinctly for ר' אליעזר: מה כרם מיוחד שהוא של חמש נפנים
239. Sic, O, S, V and Pš. According to Se it would seem as though this were the interpretation of both הירא ורך הלבב. However Tos Soṭ VII 22 where רך הלבב is separately interpreted, as well as PJ, definitely disproves it.
240. Sic. PJ

241. Sic PJ. Cf. also b 45b and j.
242. [a] I (26)note. [b] III (216) and note.
243. [a] (26) note and PJ. [b] III (209). Sic also S, V and Pš, and, of course, O and PJ.
244. V (67) and note, (68) and note, (69) and note.
245. IV (82) and note, V (148) and note.
246. I (27) note. Cf. also Malbim.
247. III (161) and note and II (37).
248. III (157) and II (37).
249. V (59) and note. Sic also O and PJ.
250. III (83). Sic O and Pš.
251. III (84). Sic PJ.
252. II (28), III (77).
253. I (35) and III (17)+(20) and notes.
254. III (37) and note.
255. [a] III (234), (235) and notes. [b] III (134), (135) and notes.
256. III (48), (49) and note, (104), (105) and note.
257. I (35) note. III (19), (20) and notes.
258. Cf. I (35) and III (17) to (22).
259. II (4) and (5). Sic PJ. V: "vestimento quod ex lana linoque contextum est". Cf. also V (9), VI (7), (8) and notes.
260. II (11) and note, V (9), VI (7), (8) and notes.
261. [a] III (242)+(243) and notes, V (88), (29) and notes.
262. Sic O.
263. V (46), (84) and (85). Sic also PJ.
264. [a] V (80)+(81) and notes, [b] V (82)+(83) and notes.
265. Sic S and O and Pš.
266. III (203). Sic V: "in domo" and PJ: לקרבא בבי מקדשא דה'
267. III (152)+(153) and note.
268. [a] II (33) note, V (51).
269. III (98). Sic V.
270. III (101) and note.
271. III (256) and note.
272. III (128)+(129) and notes.
273. V (28) and note. Cf. Malbim. Sic also O and PJ.
274. II (78), V (70) and (71).,
275. The Mishnah plays on the ground meaning of שכר.
276. III (93), (94) and notes.
277. [a] III (251) and note. Sic V. [b] V (109). Cf. also Malbim on Sa Lev XIX 10.
278. [a] III (249) and note. Sic O, PJ and Pš. [b] V (109). Cf. also Malbim on Sa Lev XIX 10.
279. Sic PJ וירבעוניה. Cf. ותפל מעל הגמל. Gen XXIV 64 which O translates ואתרכינת.
280. III (181) and IV (1) and V (130).

281. Sic Massorah, O, PJ and Pš. S and V agree with R Judah but not the division of the verses.
282. [a] III (246)+(247), and IV (5), and V (144) and note. [b] II (17) note V (8) and note.
283. III (150)+(151) and notes.
285. V (114) and note.
286. II (25), V (53) and note.
287. Sic O, J, S, V and Pš and Massorah.
288. IV (8).
289. Sic S and V.
290. III (41) and note+(182).
291. II (25), V (52) and note.
292. II (9) note.
293. III (35)+(36) and note. Sic also V: "in qualibet immunditia"
294. V (35). Sic clearly V: "nec expendi in re funebri". Cf. also Se, MT and PJ.
295. Sic PJ.
296. II (25) and note.
297. [a] III (195). [b] III (163) and note and II (37).
298. [a] III (195). [b] III (159) and II (37).
299. [a] III (190), V (96). [b] V (97).
300. [a] IV (75) and note, V (149) and note. Sic also O and PJ.
301. The verse is quoted in full in the Mishnah version of j. Cf. V(11) and the remark in b R Hash 26a and j. Cf. also J.
302. V (11) and note.
303. II (37) and note.
304. IV (3) and note. V (145)+(146) and notes. Cf. S and Pš which favor the interpretation that does not make הלוים apposites to הכהנים.
305. V (27). Sic also J, S, V and Pš.
306. Sic S, V and Pš. V (6), V (58).
307. II (7) note, (16) note, V (6).
308. Cf. b Ḥull 137a.
309. II (64) and (65) and notes V (22).
310. II (64) and (65) and notes, V (12).
311. Cf. b Ḥull 137a.
312. III (9)+(10) and notes. Sic also V.
313. II (73) and note.
314. [a] II (13) note. [b] III (199)+(200) and notes.
315. [a] V (15) and note. See also the remark of Raba in b Sabb 82b. Sic also T. [b] II (77), V (90). Sic also V.
316. III (191)+(192) and notes.
317. II (76).
318. Cf. J לאסנאה עלה בני אנשא אתקנא.
319. [a] III (245). [b] II (75).
321. II (22) and note, (23) and note.

322. VI (22) and note, (23) and note, II (44).
323. V (36).
324. II (64) and (65) and notes, V (25).
325. II (19) note.
326. [a] III (34). [b] Sic S.
327. [a] II (61), V (92). [b] Sic M: איזו היא ברית שהיא נוהגת ביום ובלילה. This is a more grammatical rendering of יומם ולילה than those of J, V, or Pš.
328. III (154)+(155) and notes.
329. IV (14) and note.
330. II (47).
331. [a] Cf. Ps XVII 3, Job VII 18.
332. [a] III (197). [b] II (83), V (91).
333. Sic also V: "fasciculum" (="bundle") like (אזוב) אגדת Ex XII 22 i. e. "that which can be grasped with five fingers".
334. [a] V (150), IV (78). [b] III (65) and note. [c] V (99), IV (79).
335. [a] V (150, IV (78). [b] III (69) and note, V (10). [c] V (99), IV (79).
336. V (17).
337. V (13).
338. I (33) note.
339. I (33) note.
340. Cf. V (55).
341. II (74) and V (93). Sic also T.
342. [a] This is different from T, S, V, and Pš which construe מכל as a comparative.
343. III (266) and note.
344. III (264) and note. This interpretation follows Maimonides who holds that R Nathan differs with anon., against Rashi.
345. [a] Cf. III (251). [b] II (10) note.
346. II (69) and V (94) and note.
347. II (82).
348. Cf. Br b Soṭ 31a where R Meir is quoted as proving that ירא אלהים may be an עובד מאהבה.
349. II (8) note. Sic also V and Pš. S must have read לו.
350. [a] apparently.
351. II (3) note. Sic also O, PJ and Pš. This interpretation follows Rashi acc. to whom the proof is from על כן עלמות אהבוך. Cf. V (40). In an unvocalized text שמניך, as Geiger would have it, would not clear up the ambiguity.
352. II (3) note. Sic also S and V.
355. III (4) and note.
356. The remark of R Judah is, according to b 103b and j, based on the word ויעתר. Tos Snh XII 11 quotes II Chr XXX 19 which contains no reference to his restoration to his kingdom.
357. III (238) and (239).

www.ingramcontent.com/pod-product-compliance
Lightning Source LLC
LaVergne TN
LVHW021553080426
835510LV00019B/2489